WeightWatchers®

Recipes in 30 minutes or less

Weekdays

D1513874

First published in Great Britain by Simon & Schuster UK Ltd, 2012
A CBS Company

Copyright © 2012, Weight Watchers International, Inc.
Simon & Schuster Illustrated Books, Simon & Schuster UK Ltd,
First Floor, 222 Gray's Inn Road, London WC1X 8HB

www.simonandschuster.co.uk

Simon & Schuster Australia, Sydney
Simon & Schuster India, New Delhi

Weight Watchers, **ProPoints** and the **ProPoints** icon are the registered
trademarks of Weight Watchers International Inc and are used under license
by Weight Watchers (UK) Ltd.

Weight Watchers Publications: Cheryl Jackson, Jane Griffiths,
Selena Makepeace, Nina McKerlie and Imogen Prescott.

Recipes written by: Sue Ashworth, Sue Beveridge, Tamsin Burnett-Hall,
Cas Clarke, Siân Davies, Roz Denny, Nicola Graimes, Becky Johnson,
Kim Morphew, Joy Skipper, Penny Stephens and Wendy Veale as well
as Weight Watchers Leaders and Members.

Photography by: Iain Bagwell, Steve Baxter, Steve Lee, Juliet Piddington
and William Shaw.
Project editor: Nicki Lampon.
Design and typesetting: Geoff Fennell.

Colour reproduction by Dot Gradations Ltd, UK.
Printed and bound in China.

A CIP catalogue for this book is available from the British Library

ISBN 978-0-85720-937-5

1 2 3 4 5 6 7 8 9 10

Pictured on the title page: Tuna with spring veg sauté p110.
Pictured on the Introduction: Spanish style garlic prawns p116, Warm pan fried duck
with fettucine p78, Syrup sponges p154.

WeightWatchers®

Recipes in 30 minutes or less

Weekdays

SIMON &
SCHUSTER
ILLUSTRATED

London · New York · Sydney · Toronto · New Delhi

A CBS COMPANY

Weight Watchers **ProPoints** Weight Loss System is a simple way to lose weight. As part of the Weight Watchers **ProPoints** plan you'll enjoy eating delicious, healthy, filling foods that help to keep you feeling satisfied for longer and in control of your portions.

Ⓥ This symbol denotes a vegetarian recipe and assumes that, where relevant, free range eggs, vegetarian cheese, vegetarian virtually fat free fromage frais, vegetarian low fat crème fraîche and vegetarian low fat yogurts are used. Virtually fat free fromage frais, low fat crème fraîche and low fat yogurts may contain traces of gelatine so they are not always vegetarian. Please check the labels.

❋ This symbol denotes a dish that can be frozen. Unless otherwise stated, you can freeze the finished dish for up to 3 months. Defrost thoroughly and reheat until the dish is piping hot throughout.

Recipe notes

Egg size: Medium sized, unless otherwise stated.

Raw eggs: Only the freshest eggs should be used. Pregnant women, the elderly and children should avoid recipes with eggs that are not fully cooked or raw.

All fruits and vegetables: Medium sized, unless otherwise stated.

Stock: Stock cubes are used in recipes, unless otherwise stated. These should be prepared according to packet instructions.

Recipe timings: These are approximate and meant to be guidelines. Please note that the preparation time includes all the steps up to and following the main cooking time(s).

Microwaves: Timings and temperatures are for a standard 800 W microwave. If necessary, adjust your own microwave.

Low fat spread: Where a recipe states to use a low fat spread, a light spread with a fat content of no less than 38% should be used.

Low fat soft cheese: Where low fat soft cheese is specified in a recipe, this refers to soft cheese with a fat content of less than 5%.

Contents

Introduction

Half an hour is all it takes to produce a tasty and healthy meal. Perfect for the busy cook, *Weekdays* is full of recipes from the best of Weight Watchers cookbooks and packed with ideas for fabulous food that you wouldn't believe you could cook so quickly.

Try a tasty Haddock Rarebit or Indian Spiced Millet for a quick lunch or light meal, feed the family in just 30 minutes with Cheat's Cottage Pie or Creamy Turkey and Pepper Fricassée, or dish up a delightful supper for two with Pan Fried Scallops followed by Pear Strudels.

So get cooking and within just 30 minutes you'll be producing beautiful food for family and friends any day of the week.

About Weight Watchers

For more than 40 years Weight Watchers has been helping people around the world to lose weight using a long term sustainable approach. Weight Watchers successful weight loss system is based on four tried and trusted principles:

- Eating healthily
- Being more active
- Adjusting behaviour to help weight loss
- Getting support in weekly meetings

Our unique **ProPoints** system empowers you to manage your food plan and make wise recipe choices for a healthier, happier you. To find out more about Weight Watchers and the **ProPoints** values for these recipes contact Customer Services on 0845 345 1500.

Storing and freezing

Making meals ahead of time and storing or freezing them is one of the keys to producing healthy tasty meals during a busy week. Many dishes store well in the fridge, but make sure you use them up within a day or two. Some can also be frozen. Try making double the quantity when you cook a recipe and storing the extra portions in the freezer. This way you'll always have a fantastic selection of meals that you can pull out and reheat at the end of a busy day. However, it is important to make sure you know how to freeze safely.

- Wrap any food to be frozen in rigid containers or strong freezer bags. This is important to stop foods contaminating each other or getting freezer burn.
- Label the containers or bags with the contents and date – your freezer should have a star marking that tells you how long you can keep different types of frozen food.
- Never freeze warm food – always let it cool completely first.
- Never freeze food that has already been frozen and defrosted.
- Freeze food in portions, then you can take out as little or as much as you need each time.
- Defrost what you need in the fridge, making sure you put anything that might have juices, such as meat, on a covered plate or in a container.

- Fresh food, such as raw meat and fish, should be wrapped and frozen as soon as possible.
- Most fruit and vegetables can be frozen by open freezing. Lay them out on a tray, freeze until solid and then pack them into bags.
- Some vegetables, such as peas, broccoli and broad beans can be blanched first by cooking for 2 minutes in boiling water. Drain, refresh under cold water and then freeze once cold.

- Fresh herbs are great frozen – either seal leaves in bags or, for soft herbs such as basil and parsley, chop finely and add to ice cube trays with water. These are great for dropping into casseroles or soups straight from the freezer.

Some things cannot be frozen. Whole eggs do not freeze well, but yolks and whites can be frozen separately. Vegetables with a high water content, such as salad leaves, celery and cucumber, will not freeze. Fried foods will be soggy if frozen, and sauces such as mayonnaise will separate when thawed and should not be frozen.

Shopping hints and tips

Always buy the best ingredients you can afford. If you are going to cook healthy meals, it is worth investing in some quality ingredients that will really add flavour to your dishes. When buying meat, choose lean cuts of meat or lean mince, and if you are buying prepacked cooked sliced meat, buy it fresh from the deli counter.

When you're going around the supermarket it's tempting to pick up foods you like and put them in your trolley without thinking about how you will use them. So, a good plan is to decide what dishes you want to cook before you go shopping, check your store cupboard and make a list of what you need. You'll save time by not drifting aimlessly around the supermarket picking up what you fancy.

We've added a checklist here for some of the store cupboard ingredients used in this book. Just add fresh ingredients in your regular shop and you'll be ready to cook the wonderful recipes in *Weekdays*.

Store cupboard checklist

- [ ] apricots, canned in natural juice
- [ ] artificial sweetener
- [ ] baking powder
- [ ] black beans, canned
- [ ] cannellini beans, canned
- [ ] cardamom pods
- [ ] chick peas, canned
- [ ] chilli (flakes and powder)
- [ ] chilli sauce
- [ ] chocolate (70% cocoa solids)
- [ ] cinnamon, ground
- [ ] cocoa powder
- [ ] coconut milk, reduced fat
- [ ] cooking spray, calorie controlled
- [ ] coriander (seeds and ground)
- [ ] cornflour
- [ ] crab meat, canned in brine
- [ ] cumin (seeds and ground)
- [ ] curry (paste and powder)
- [ ] fish sauce
- [ ] flour (plain and self raising)
- [ ] garam masala
- [ ] garlic purée
- [ ] golden syrup
- [ ] harissa paste
- [ ] herbs, dried (mixed and Italian)
- [ ] hoisin sauce
- [ ] honey, runny
- [ ] jam, reduced sugar
- [ ] kidney beans, canned
- [ ] lentils, dried red
- [ ] lime leaves, dried
- [ ] mayonnaise, extra light
- [ ] millet grain, dried
- [ ] mustard (Dijon and wholegrain)
- [ ] mustard seeds
- [ ] noodles (dried and fresh)
- [ ] oil, olive
- [ ] olives in brine, black
- [ ] passata
- [ ] pasta, dried
- [ ] peppercorns
- [ ] peppers, piquante in a jar
- [ ] pesto sauce
- [ ] pineapple rings, canned in natural juice
- [ ] rice, dried (basmati and long grain)
- [ ] saffron
- [ ] salt
- [ ] soy sauce
- [ ] stock cubes
- [ ] sugar (caster and soft brown)
- [ ] sweetcorn, canned
- [ ] Tabasco sauce
- [ ] teriyaki sauce
- [ ] tomato purée
- [ ] tomatoes, canned
- [ ] tomatoes, sun-dried in a jar
- [ ] vanilla essence
- [ ] vinegar, balsamic
- [ ] Worcestershire sauce

Lunches and light bites

Steak and onion sandwich

Serves 1
351 calories per serving
Takes 15 minutes

80 g (3 oz) lean minute or frying steak, visible fat removed

calorie controlled cooking spray

½ small red onion, sliced thinly

1 tablespoon balsamic vinegar

2 medium slices granary bread

salt and freshly ground black pepper

a handful of rocket, to serve

Piling hot meat on to bread is always a favourite and this minute steak with balsamic fried onions is fast and tasty.

1 Season the steak on both sides. Lightly coat a small non stick frying pan with the cooking spray and heat until hot. Add the steak and cook, turning once, for 2–3 minutes until beginning to brown. Remove from the pan and keep warm.

2 Spray the pan again with the cooking spray and, when hot, add the onion. Cook over a medium heat for 5 minutes until soft and browned. Stir in the balsamic vinegar and remove from the heat.

3 Place the steak on one of the slices of bread and top with the onion and pan juices, followed by the rocket and the other slice of bread.

Tip... If you prefer, use a 110 g (4 oz) piece of French baguette instead.

Indian spiced millet

Serves 2
352 calories per serving
Takes 10 minutes to prepare,
  15 minutes to cook

100 g (3½ oz) dried millet
  grain
300 ml (10 fl oz) hot chicken
  stock
4 freeze dried curry leaves
1 egg
1 small red onion, chopped
  finely
1 small red chilli, de-seeded
  and sliced finely
2 teaspoons black or yellow
  mustard seeds
1 teaspoon garam masala
50 g (1¾ oz) baby spinach
  leaves, washed and
  shredded roughly
100 g (3½ oz) cooked skinless
  chicken breast fillet, cut into
  bite size pieces

*Similar to couscous and bulgar wheat, millet grain is a
very versatile cereal. It's available at most supermarkets
or health food shops but, if you can't find it, use the same
amount of bulgar wheat.*

1 Put the millet grain in a lidded saucepan with the hot chicken
stock and curry leaves. Bring to the boil, cover and simmer for
12–15 minutes until tender and all the stock has been absorbed.

2 Meanwhile, bring a small saucepan of water to the boil, add
the egg and simmer for 5–6 minutes. Drain and plunge into
cold water.

3 Transfer the millet grain to a bowl and stir in the onion, chilli,
mustard seeds, garam masala, spinach and chicken. Divide the
salad between two plates.

4 Peel the egg, cut in half and put on top of each salad. Serve
immediately.

Crabayo bruschetta

Serves 2
445 calories per serving
Takes 15 minutes

170 g can white crab meat in brine, drained

2 tablespoons reduced fat mayonnaise

grated zest and juice of ½ a lime

1 tablespoon finely chopped fresh coriander

a generous pinch of dried chilli flakes

150 g (5½ oz) ciabatta, cut in half lengthways

calorie controlled cooking spray

freshly ground black pepper

To serve

50 g (1¾ oz) cucumber, de-seeded and sliced finely

2 spring onions, shredded

If you're on the move, cook the ciabatta and wrap it in foil. Spoon the crab mixture into a sealable container and then serve when needed. For an easy lunch, use half the crab mixture to fill two medium slices of wholemeal bread.

1 Mix together the crab meat, mayonnaise, lime zest and juice, coriander, chilli flakes and freshly ground black pepper in a bowl. Set aside.

2 Cut each of the ciabatta halves in half again and spray with the cooking spray. Heat a griddle pan or non stick frying pan until hot and cook the ciabatta slices for 3–4 minutes on one side until charred. Turn over and cook on the other side for a further 3–4 minutes. Remove from the pan and top each slice with some of the crab mixture. Top with the cucumber and spring onions and serve immediately.

Variation... Why not try using a drained 200 g can of tuna steak in brine, instead of the crab?

Smoked turkey and spinach wrap

Serves 2
318 calories per serving
Takes 20 minutes

100 g (3½ oz) baby spinach, washed
100 g (3½ oz) smoked turkey breast slices
2 medium flour tortillas

For the red onion relish
calorie controlled cooking spray
2 large onions, sliced thinly
125 ml (4 fl oz) red wine
a few fresh thyme sprigs, chopped
salt and freshly ground black pepper

This tortilla sandwich makes a great lunch on the run, or it can be sliced into rounds and served as a canapé or starter.

1 First make the relish. Heat a non stick frying pan and spray with the cooking spray. Add the onions and stir fry for 5 minutes until softened. Add the wine and thyme, season and bring to the boil. Simmer gently for 10 minutes until most of the wine has evaporated and the onions are soft.

2 To assemble the wraps, place half the spinach and turkey on each tortilla, spoon 2 teaspoons of the relish over and roll up to serve.

Tip... Smoked turkey breast slices are available in the prepacked cooked meat section of most supermarkets.

Variations... Alternatives to smoked turkey are roast turkey or cooked chicken slices.

Feta salad in seconds

Serves 4
244 calories per serving
Takes 5 minutes

**1 large bag mixed salad
leaves with herbs**
12 cherry tomatoes, halved
**400 g (14 oz) mild piquante
peppers in a jar**
75 g (2¾ oz) Feta cheese
**finely grated zest and juice
of a lemon**
2 tablespoons olive oil
a few drops of Tabasco sauce
**salt and freshly ground black
pepper**

This is a fast and simple version of the recipe on page 39.

1 Divide the salad leaves and cherry tomatoes between four serving plates. Drain the peppers, tear them into strips and divide between the leaves.

2 Crumble the Feta over the salads.

3 Mix the lemon zest and lemon juice with the olive oil. Add a few drops of Tabasco sauce and season. Sprinkle over the salads and serve at once.

Grilled halloumi on salad leaves

Serves 4
178 calories per serving
Takes 15 minutes

4 medium slices wholemeal bread
80 g (3 oz) halloumi cheese, sliced into 8 thin slices
180 g (6½ oz) mixed salad leaves

For the dressing
2 teaspoons olive oil
grated zest and juice of a lemon
1 fresh rosemary sprig, chopped finely
a small bunch of fresh parsley, chopped finely
1 garlic clove, crushed

Halloumi is a Cypriot cheese that has a distinctive elastic texture and salty taste. It is at its best when grilled but must be eaten immediately as it quickly becomes rubbery.

1 Preheat the grill to medium and toast the bread on one side under the grill.

2 Put two slices of halloumi on the untoasted side of each slice of bread and grill for 1–2 minutes until golden and bubbling. Cut each slice of bread into four.

3 Divide the salad leaves between four serving plates, whisk together the dressing ingredients and then spoon over the salads.

4 Top the salads with the grilled cheese croûtons and eat immediately.

Spicy rice salad

Serves 4
263 calories per serving
Takes 30 minutes

200 g (7 oz) dried long grain brown rice

a generous pinch of saffron threads

1 teaspoon cumin seeds

1 teaspoon coriander seeds

2 cardamom pods, seeds removed and retained

1 teaspoon mild chilli powder

2 large tomatoes, de-seeded and diced finely

1 roasted red pepper from a jar, drained, rinsed and diced finely

25 g packet fresh coriander, chopped roughly

½ red onion, chopped finely

juice of a lemon

3 tablespoons 0% fat Greek yogurt

This rice salad is perfect with any barbecued food, cold meats or lunchboxes.

1 Bring a large lidded saucepan of water to the boil, add the rice and saffron and cook according to the packet instructions until tender.

2 Meanwhile, crush the cumin, coriander and cardamom seeds with a pestle and mortar. Put into a large bowl and mix together with the chilli powder, tomatoes, pepper, coriander, onion and lemon juice.

3 Drain the rice and rinse in cold water until cold. Drain again thoroughly using the base of a bowl to squeeze out any excess water. Add to the tomato mixture along with the yogurt. Mix together really well to ensure everything is coated. Serve immediately.

Kidney bean and roasted pepper wraps

Serves 4

233 calories per serving

Takes 10 minutes to prepare,
20 minutes to cook

1 red pepper, de-seeded and
diced

1 green pepper, de-seeded
and diced

2 garlic cloves, crushed

calorie controlled cooking
spray

300 g (10½ oz) canned kidney
beans, drained and rinsed

1 tablespoon sweet chilli
sauce

finely grated zest of a lime

4 medium flour tortillas

2 tablespoons chopped fresh
coriander

salt and freshly ground black
pepper

*These delightful spicy wraps make a tasty alternative to
sandwiches. Make up the filling beforehand, allowing it
to cool before filling each tortilla wrap.*

1 Preheat the oven to Gas Mark 6/200°C/fan oven 180°C.
Line a roasting tin with foil. Place the peppers in the tin and
then mix in the garlic. Spray with the cooking spray, season
and roast for 15 minutes.

2 Remove the tin from the oven and add the kidney beans,
sweet chilli sauce and lime zest. Return to the oven for a
further 5 minutes.

3 Meanwhile, warm the tortillas according to the packet
instructions.

4 Sprinkle the coriander over the kidney bean mixture, spoon
the filling equally between the tortillas and then roll them up.
Slice the tortillas diagonally in half and arrange them on a
serving plate.

Variation... If you like, top the filling of each tortilla with
a tablespoon of half fat crème fraîche.

Spinach, black olive and tomato pizzas

Serves 4
156 calories per serving
Takes 20 minutes

2 English muffins, halved
2 tablespoons sun-dried tomato paste
½ teaspoon dried mixed herbs
150 g (5½ oz) baby spinach, washed
1 beefsteak tomato, sliced
25 g (1 oz) stoned black olives, halved
50 g (1¾ oz) light mozzarella cheese, thinly sliced
salt and freshly ground black pepper

These are perfect for a light meal – full of flavour and colour.

1 Preheat the grill to medium and lightly toast the muffin halves on both sides.

2 Mix together the tomato paste and mixed herbs. Spread on to one side of each muffin half.

3 Place the spinach in a large lidded saucepan, cover tightly and cook for 2 minutes until wilted. Drain, squeezing out any excess moisture, and arrange on top of the pizza with a slice of tomato, a few olive halves and the sliced mozzarella.

4 Season well and return to the grill for 2–3 minutes, until the cheese has melted.

Spiced beef kebabs

Serves 2
201 calories per serving
Takes 10 minutes to prepare
+ marinating, 8–10 minutes
to cook

juice of a small lemon
1 teaspoon medium curry
powder
¼ teaspoon dried mint
250 g (9 oz) rump steak,
visible fat removed, cut into
2.5 cm (1 inch) cubes
1 red onion, chopped roughly
1 red pepper, de-seeded and
chopped roughly
salt and freshly ground black
pepper

Serve these mildly spiced beef kebabs on a bed of crisp
mixed salad, accompanied by 1 tablespoon of low fat
natural yogurt per person.

1 Preheat the grill to its highest setting.

2 Mix the lemon juice, curry powder and mint together in a
bowl and season. Stir in the diced steak, red onion and pepper
and mix well to coat in the spice mixture.

3 Thread the cubes of spiced beef on to skewers, alternating
with the pepper and red onion. Grill for 8–10 minutes, turning
once or twice, until cooked to your liking.

Tip... If using wooden skewers, soak them in water for
20 minutes beforehand to prevent them from burning.

Variation... You can also use 2 x 125 g (4½ oz) skinless
boneless chicken breasts in place of the rump steak.

Leeks and crispy ham salad

Serves 2

78 calories per serving

Takes 10 minutes to prepare, 15 minutes to cook

8 baby leeks or 2 leeks, halved and halved again lengthways

100 g (3½ oz) tomatoes, quartered

calorie controlled cooking spray

1 tablespoon balsamic vinegar

1 teaspoon caster sugar

2 thin slices Parma ham

salt and freshly ground black pepper

A light and healthy starter, lunch or accompaniment to grilled fish.

1 Bring a large saucepan of water to the boil, add the leeks and blanch for 4–8 minutes depending on their size and tenderness. Check with the point of a sharp knife to see if they are tender.

2 Meanwhile, preheat the oven to Gas Mark 7/220°C/fan oven 200°C. Place the tomato quarters on a baking tray. Season, spray with the cooking spray and then roast for 10 minutes, until softened and slightly charred.

3 Put the tomatoes in a blender with the vinegar and sugar, or use a hand held blender, and blend to a vinaigrette. Push through a sieve to remove all the seeds.

4 Preheat the grill to medium and grill the Parma ham for 2 minutes until curled and crispy. Arrange the leeks on two serving plates, pour the tomato vinaigrette over, top with a piece of crispy ham and serve.

Tip... If they are available, baby leeks make this salad especially good, as they are so tender and sweet.

Variation... Use 2 x 25 g (1 oz) lean back bacon rashers, grilled and then chopped and sprinkled over, instead of the Parma ham.

Haddock rarebit

Serves 2

407 calories per serving

Takes 15 minutes to prepare,
15 minutes to cook

2 x 200 g (7 oz) smoked
haddock fillets

400 g (14 oz) frozen chopped
spinach

75 g (2¾ oz) half fat Cheddar
cheese, grated

2 tablespoons low fat
mayonnaise

½ teaspoon mustard powder

1 teaspoon Worcestershire
sauce

a few drops of Tabasco sauce

½ teaspoon grated nutmeg

salt and freshly ground black
pepper

This fish dish is perfect for a light lunch or supper.

1 Put the haddock fillets into a non stick frying pan and add
200 ml (7 fl oz) of water. Poach gently for about 6–8 minutes
until the fish is cooked; the flesh should be opaque and flake
easily.

2 Meanwhile, cook the spinach according to the packet
instructions, squeeze out the excess moisture and then
transfer to two individual shallow flameproof dishes. Season.

3 Remove the skin from the haddock and lay one fillet on top
of the spinach in each dish. Preheat the grill to medium-high.

4 Mix the cheese with the mayonnaise, mustard powder,
Worcestershire sauce, Tabasco sauce and nutmeg. Spread this
mixture over the fish fillets to cover them completely. Grill until
browned and bubbling and serve at once.

Tip... The dish can be finished off in the oven instead of
under the grill. Simply bake for about 5–6 minutes at Gas
Mark 6/200°C/fan oven 180°C.

Variation... For a 'Buck Haddock Rarebit', add a poached
egg and serve it on top of the fish and cheese.

Peppery pesto pasta

Serves 4
312 calories per serving
Takes 15 minutes

250 g (9 oz) dried spaghetti
2 tablespoons pine nut kernels
30 g (1¼ oz) rocket
1 tablespoon extra virgin
  olive oil
1 garlic clove, chopped
  roughly
**salt and freshly ground black
  pepper**
10 g (¼ oz) Parmesan cheese,
  grated finely, to serve

*This quick home made pesto is flavourful and really easy
to make.*

1 Bring a large saucepan of water to the boil, add the pasta
and cook according to the packet instructions.

2 Meanwhile, gently brown the pine nut kernels in a non stick
pan until they are golden all over.

3 Place the rocket, olive oil, garlic and 1 tablespoon of water
in a food processor, or use a hand held blender, and whizz
until a rough paste forms. Add the pine nut kernels and blend
so that they form the pesto. Season.

4 Drain the pasta, reserving 2 tablespoons of the cooking
liquid. Return to the pan with the reserved liquid, add the pesto
and toss until well combined. Serve hot, sprinkled with the
Parmesan cheese.

*Tip... The pesto will keep covered in the fridge for up to
5 days.*

Beany beef

Serves 2
247 calories per serving
Takes 5 minutes

1 teaspoon Dijon mustard
1 teaspoon wholegrain
mustard
50 g (1¾ oz) low fat fromage
frais
30 g (1¼ oz) low fat soft
cheese with garlic and herbs
410 g can cannellini beans,
drained and rinsed
50 g (1¾ oz) roasted red
peppers, drained, de-seeded
and diced
1 Little Gem lettuce, shredded
finely
2 tablespoons snipped fresh
salad cress
75 g (2¾ oz) sliced roast beef
freshly ground black pepper

If you prepare this the night before for a packed lunch,
don't mix the lettuce and cress through until the morning.

1 In a bowl, mix together both mustards, the fromage frais,
soft cheese and freshly ground black pepper.

2 Add the cannellini beans, pepper, lettuce and cress and gently
fold to combine. Divide between two plates and top with folds
of the sliced beef.

Ⓥ Variation... You can replace the beef with chargrilled
slices of aubergine and courgette.

Turkey and pepper salad

Serves 4
256 calories per serving
Takes 10 minutes

8 x 25 g (1 oz) **turkey rashers**
1 large bag **mixed salad leaves with herbs**
12 **cherry tomatoes**, halved
400 g (14 oz) **mild piquante peppers in a jar**
finely grated zest and juice of a lemon
2 tablespoons **olive oil**
a few drops of Tabasco sauce
salt and freshly ground black pepper

Prepacked mixed salad leaves are very convenient and they give you loads of ideas for stylish salads.

1 Preheat the grill to hot.

2 Arrange the turkey rashers on the grill rack. Grill for 2 minutes on each side. Remove and drain on kitchen towel.

3 Divide the salad leaves and cherry tomatoes between four serving plates. Snip the turkey rashers into pieces and sprinkle them over the salad leaves. Drain the peppers, tear them into strips and divide between the salads.

4 Mix the lemon zest and lemon juice with the olive oil. Add a few drops of Tabasco sauce and season. Sprinkle over the salads and serve at once.

❤ Variation... For a tasty vegetarian version, see the recipe on page 22.

Warm broad bean and smoked ham pittas

Serves 4
262 calories per serving
Takes 10 minutes

300 g (10½ oz) broad beans
calorie controlled cooking
spray
1 onion, sliced finely
1 red chilli, de-seeded and
chopped finely
2 garlic cloves, crushed
1 tablespoon balsamic vinegar
50 g (1¾ oz) smoked ham, cut
into small strips
a small bunch of fresh mint,
chopped
2 tablespoons virtually fat free
fromage frais
4 pitta breads
salt and freshly ground black
pepper

This summery salad can be served as an accompaniment
to fish or meat or stuffed into a pitta pocket as suggested
in this recipe.

1 Bring a saucepan of water to the boil, add the broad beans and cook for about 5 minutes or until tender. Drain and slip them from their skins to reveal the bright green beans.

2 Heat a non stick frying pan and spray with the cooking spray. Add the onion, chilli and garlic and cook for a few minutes, until softened and golden.

3 Remove the pan from the heat and add the balsamic vinegar, ham, broad beans, mint and fromage frais. Season and mix together gently.

4 Warm the pitta breads in the oven or toaster. Spoon the ham and bean mixture into the pittas and serve.

Marvellous meat

Balsamic glazed lamb with parsnip purée

Serves 4
353 calories per serving
Takes 20 minutes

700 g (1 lb 9 oz) parsnips, peeled and chopped roughly
4 x 100 g (3½ oz) lean lamb leg steaks, visible fat removed
calorie controlled cooking spray
1 red onion, sliced
½ teaspoon dried rosemary
2 tablespoons balsamic vinegar
2 tablespoons redcurrant jelly
4 tablespoons skimmed milk
salt and freshly ground black pepper

This is wonderful served with rocket.

1 Bring a saucepan of water to the boil, add the parsnips and cook for 10 minutes or until soft.

2 Meanwhile, heat a non stick frying pan and season the lamb steaks. Spray the frying pan with the cooking spray and add the lamb. Scatter the red onion around the lamb and sprinkle in the rosemary. Cook for 3 minutes on each side over a high heat, stirring the onions around when you turn the lamb.

3 Add the balsamic vinegar, redcurrant jelly and 2 tablespoons of water to the frying pan. Bubble for 2 minutes, turning the lamb to glaze it in the sauce.

4 Drain the parsnips and mash with the milk. Serve the parsnip purée with the lamb steaks and spoon the red onions and sauce over the top.

Chinese pork parcels

Serves 4

320 calories per serving

Takes 20 minutes

100 g (3½ oz) dried easy cook rice

450 g (1 lb) pork mince

2 garlic cloves, chopped

1–2 teaspoons ginger purée

2 tablespoons soy sauce, plus extra for dipping

4 spring onions, chopped

200 g (7 oz) beansprouts

1 large carrot, peeled and grated

freshly ground black pepper

1 Iceberg lettuce, whole leaves separated, to serve

Try this nifty way with pork mince for an economical midweek meal.

1 Bring a saucepan of water to the boil, add the rice and cook according to the packet instructions.

2 Meanwhile, heat a large non stick frying pan and dry fry the pork for 5 minutes until lightly coloured and crumbly. Stir in the garlic and ginger and cook for a further 5 minutes to ensure the pork is well done.

3 Stir in the soy sauce, spring onions, beansprouts and carrot and season with black pepper. Cook for 2–3 minutes.

4 Drain the rice thoroughly and stir into the pork. Arrange two whole lettuce leaves on each plate. Divide the mince mixture between them, roll each leaf up and enjoy with additional soy sauce, for dipping.

Cheat's cottage pie

Serves 4
368 calories per serving
Takes 30 minutes
❄

500 g (1 lb 2 oz) potatoes, peeled and diced
calorie controlled cooking spray
1 large onion, grated
1 carrot, peeled and cut into small dice
2 garlic cloves, chopped
500 g (1 lb 2 oz) lean beef mince
400 g can chopped tomatoes
1 tablespoon tomato purée
2 teaspoons dried mixed herbs
1 teaspoon Worcestershire sauce
salt and freshly ground black pepper

This quick version of a family favourite is cooked entirely on the hob. Serve with green vegetables, such as broccoli and green beans.

1 Bring a saucepan of water to the boil, add the potatoes and cook for 10–15 minutes until tender.

2 Meanwhile, heat a large, lidded, non stick frying pan, spray with the cooking spray and fry the onion and carrot for 7 minutes, stirring frequently and adding a splash of water if they start to stick. Add the garlic and mince and brown for 3 minutes.

3 Stir in the chopped tomatoes, tomato purée, herbs and Worcestershire sauce. Season and simmer for 15 minutes, stirring regularly. Cover with a lid if the sauce starts to get dry.

4 Drain the potatoes, season and mash until smooth. Divide the mince between four bowls and top with a dollop of mash and freshly ground black pepper before serving.

Creamy mushroom pork

Serves 4
255 calories per serving
Takes 30 minutes

calorie controlled cooking
  spray
125 g (4½ oz) chestnut
  mushrooms, sliced
1 garlic clove, crushed
300 ml (10 fl oz) vegetable
  stock
100 g (3½ oz) low fat soft
  cheese
1 tablespoon chopped fresh
  tarragon
4 x 125 g (4½ oz) pork loin
  steaks, visible fat removed

*Pork loin steaks are low in fat and although this sauce
looks and tastes really creamy, it uses low fat soft cheese.
Try adding 1 tablespoon of wholegrain mustard to the
sauce instead of the tarragon, and serve with cooked
courgettes.*

1 Lightly spray a non stick saucepan with the cooking spray
and, when sizzling, add the mushrooms. Cook over a medium
heat until the mushroom juices have evaporated, about
7 minutes.

2 Add the garlic and stock and boil for 3 minutes until reduced
by about a third. Whisk in the soft cheese and tarragon. Remove
from the heat.

3 Preheat the grill to medium and cook the pork steaks for
8–10 minutes, turning once, until golden and cooked through.

4 Warm the sauce and serve spooned over the steaks.

Burgers with spicy salsa

Serves 4
261 calories per serving
Takes 30 minutes
❄

**calorie controlled cooking
    spray**

For the burgers
250 g (9 oz) lean beef mince
2 courgettes, grated
2 carrots, peeled and grated
1 large onion, chopped finely
2 garlic cloves, crushed
**1 red pepper, de-seeded and
    chopped**
2 teaspoons English mustard
**2 medium slices bread, made
    into breadcrumbs**
1 egg
**salt and freshly ground black
    pepper**

For the spicy salsa
**6 plum tomatoes, quartered,
    de-seeded and diced finely**
1 small red onion, diced finely
**1 small red chilli, de-seeded
    and diced finely**
juice of a lime
2 teaspoons balsamic vinegar

*Tasting these burgers you would never guess that they
are packed full of vegetables. Serve in a medium burger
bun per person with lots of crisp lettuce.*

1 Mix together all the ingredients for the burgers. Take
tablespoonfuls of the mixture and, using wet hands, form
into eight patties.

2 Heat a non stick frying pan, spray with the cooking spray
and fry the patties in batches for 3–4 minutes on each side
until cooked through. Remove from the pan and set aside,
covered with foil to keep warm while you cook the remaining
patties.

3 Make the salsa by mixing all the ingredients together and
serve with the burgers.

Tip... These burgers can also be cooked on a chargrill or
barbecue for a smokey flavour.

Stir fried beef with black bean sauce

Serves 4

161 calories per serving

Takes 10 minutes to prepare,
15–20 minutes to cook

**calorie controlled cooking
spray**

**300 g (10½ oz) lean beef fillet
steak, cut into small bite
size pieces**

1 onion, sliced

2 garlic cloves, crushed

**2 cm (¾ inch) fresh root
ginger, chopped**

**1 yellow pepper, de-seeded
and sliced**

**150 g (5½ oz) green beans,
trimmed and cut in half**

**4 tablespoons black bean
sauce**

*Stir frying is so quick, and with lots of great sauces
available it's the perfect way to make a delicious meal.
Serve with steamed pak choi.*

1 Heat a wok or large non stick frying pan and spray with
the cooking spray. Add the pieces of beef and stir fry for
5–6 minutes, until browned. Remove with a slotted spoon.

2 Add the onion, garlic and ginger to the wok or pan and stir
fry for 4–5 minutes before adding the pepper and green
beans. Stir fry for another 2–3 minutes.

3 Return the beef to the wok or pan with the black bean
sauce and 100 ml (3½ fl oz) of water.

4 Stir fry for another 5–6 minutes, until the beef is cooked
and the sauce has thickened.

❤ **Variation...** For a fantastic vegetarian version, see the
recipe on page 127.

Pork meat loaf

Serves 4

270 calories per serving

Takes 5 minutes to prepare,
   25 minutes to cook

❄

1 medium slice white or
   wholemeal bread, crusts
   removed

500 g (1 lb 2 oz) pork mince

2 teaspoons garlic purée

1 teaspoon fine sea salt

½ teaspoon dried mixed herbs

**2 tablespoons spicy brown
   sauce**

**calorie controlled cooking
   spray**

**2 x 25 g (1 oz) streaky bacon
   rashers**

freshly ground black pepper

Minced pork is marvellously lean nowadays and is excellent used in this hot family style spicy meat loaf.

1 Plunge the bread slice into a bowl of cold water and then remove it and squeeze it dry. Place the wet bread in a large bowl and break it up with a fork.

2 Add the pork, garlic purée, sea salt, dried mixed herbs and brown sauce. Season with black pepper and mix it all together thoroughly. Preheat the oven to Gas Mark 6/200°C/fan oven 180°C.

3 Place a large sheet of foil on the base of a shallow roasting tin and spray it evenly with the cooking spray. Cut the bacon rashers in half and place them in the centre of the foil.

4 Mound the minced pork mixture on top of the bacon, pressing and shaping it into a thick roll and wrapping the bacon around the mixture. Draw the foil sides up and scrunch them loosely together.

5 Bake the loaf in the oven for about 20 minutes, until the meat feels firm when pressed. Allow it to stand for 5 minutes. Serve the meat loaf in thick slices with any remaining cooking juices strained and poured over.

Tip... Freeze separate slices wrapped in cling film to eat another time.

Variation... Try 500 g (1 lb 2 oz) of turkey or chicken mince instead of the pork.

Lazy lamb and lentils

Serves 4

261 calories per serving

Takes 10 minutes to prepare,
  20 minutes to cook

❄

350 g (12 oz) lean lamb, cut
  into 2 cm (¾ inch) pieces

1 onion, chopped

2 teaspoons garlic purée

2 teaspoons harissa paste

100 g (3½ oz) dried red lentils

200 g (7 oz) canned chopped
  tomatoes

300 ml (10 fl oz) hot lamb or
  chicken stock

2 tablespoons chopped fresh
  parsley

salt and freshly ground black
  pepper

This dish is 'lazy' since it needs so little preparation or attention.

1 Heat a large, lidded, non stick saucepan and dry fry the lamb for 5 minutes, until lightly browned all over.

2 Add the onion, garlic and harissa paste and continue to cook for a further 3–4 minutes. Add the lentils, tomatoes and stock. Bring to the boil, cover and simmer for 20 minutes, or until the lentils are tender and the stock is nearly all absorbed.

3 Stir in the parsley, check the seasoning and serve.

Tip... Lentils can often be used in place of meat in recipes. They are also delicious in soups too, so it's a good idea to keep a packet of red lentils, which don't need pre-soaking, in your store cupboard.

Somerset sausage casserole

Serves 4

243 calories per serving

Takes 10 minutes to prepare,
20 minutes to cook

❄

450 g (1 lb) low fat pork sausages

2 leeks, sliced

2 celery sticks, sliced

2 carrots, peeled and sliced thinly

1 green pepper, de-seeded and sliced

400 g can chopped tomatoes with herbs

1 tablespoon tomato purée

150 ml (5 fl oz) dry cider

1 tablespoon cornflour

175 g (6 oz) open mushrooms, sliced

1 tablespoon chopped fresh sage or 1 teaspoon dried sage

salt and freshly ground black pepper

This is great served with 60 g (2 oz) of dried pasta per person, cooked according to the packet instructions.

1 Heat a large, lidded, non stick saucepan and dry fry the sausages for 2–3 minutes, turning frequently. Add the leeks, celery, carrots and pepper. Cover and cook, shaking the pan every now and then, for a further 2–3 minutes.

2 Pour over the tomatoes, tomato purée and cider. Bring to the boil, cover and simmer for 10 minutes.

3 Blend the cornflour with 3 tablespoons of water and stir into the casserole together with the mushrooms and sage. Simmer, uncovered, for a further 10 minutes. Season to taste and serve.

Tip... Don't forget to make good use of your food processor for speedy chopping and slicing vegetables if you have one.

Variations... Replace the cider with the same quantity of apple juice.

♥ For a vegetarian version, use a 250 g packet of Quorn sausages.

Steak au poivre with oven sautéed potatoes

Serves 2
517 calories per serving
Takes 30 minutes

**calorie controlled cooking
spray**

For the oven sautéed potatoes
**400 g (14 oz) potatoes, peeled
and diced**
**1 tablespoon chopped fresh
rosemary**
a pinch of coarse sea salt

For the steak au poivre
**½ teaspoon black
peppercorns, crushed
coarsely**
**2 x 175 g (6 oz) rump steaks,
visible fat removed**
2 shallots, chopped finely
100 ml (3½ fl oz) red wine
100 ml (3½ fl oz) beef stock
salt

*These crispy oven sautéed potatoes are a tasty alternative
to chips – perfect with a juicy steak. Serve with fine green
beans for a traditional French accompaniment.*

1 Preheat the oven to Gas Mark 6/200°C/fan oven 180°C.

2 Bring a saucepan of water to the boil, add the potatoes and
cook for 5 minutes. Drain well. Shake around in the pan to
roughen the edges slightly and then spread them out on a
non stick baking tray and lightly coat with the cooking spray.
Roast for 20 minutes until golden and crisp.

3 Meanwhile, press the peppercorns into the steaks and
season with a little salt. Heat a non stick frying pan until really
hot, spray with the cooking spray and add the steaks. Sprinkle
the shallots around the steaks. Cook the steaks for 2 minutes
on each side for medium rare or 3 minutes on each side for
well done.

4 About 2 minutes before the end of the cooking time, add the
wine and stock to the pan and allow it to boil until reduced and
slightly syrupy.

5 Toss the potatoes with the rosemary and some coarse sea
salt and serve with the steaks and sauce.

Tip... Part cooking the potatoes and shaking them in the
pan to roughen the edges before roasting helps to give a
really crispy result. The same trick works well for roast
potatoes.

Spicy chorizo farfalle

Serves 4
336 calories per serving
Takes 25 minutes

150 g (5½ oz) chorizo sausage, sliced
1 red pepper, de-seeded and sliced
1 green pepper, de-seeded and sliced
1 yellow pepper, de-seeded and sliced
500 g (1 lb 2 oz) passata
150 g (5½ oz) dried farfalle
185 g can black olives in brine, drained and stoned

A simple, but colourful and tasty pasta dish that can be whipped up in no time at all.

1 Heat a large non stick frying pan and dry fry the chorizo and peppers for 3–5 minutes until beginning to brown. Add the passata and simmer for 10 minutes, adding a little water if the sauce gets too thick.

2 Meanwhile, bring a large saucepan of water to the boil, add the pasta and cook according to the packet instructions. Drain.

3 Toss the olives into the pasta and serve with the sauce on top.

Indian lamb pizza

Serves 2
430 calories per serving
Takes 20 minutes

calorie controlled cooking
  spray
100 g (3½ oz) lean lamb mince
½ small onion, chopped finely
1 teaspoon ground cumin
1 teaspoon ground coriander
140 g (5 oz) plain naan
2 tablespoons low fat soft
  cheese
1 small sprig of fresh mint,
  chopped roughly
15 g (½ oz) toasted flaked
  almonds

*When you fancy a curry but are short of time, these pizzas
will hit the spot. Serve with 1 tablespoon of mango chutney
per person and a generous mixed salad.*

1 Preheat the oven to Gas Mark 5/190°C/fan oven 170°C.
Heat a non stick frying pan and spray with the cooking spray.
Add the lamb and cook until browned, stirring to break it up.

2 Add the onion, ground cumin and coriander and cook for
3 minutes until the onion is browned, breaking up the lamb
and stirring constantly with a wooden spoon. Remove from
the heat.

3 Carefully slice the naan in half through the middle (like
opening a pitta) so you get two thin naans and put on a large
baking tray. Spread half of the soft cheese over one side of
each naan and top with the lamb mixture. Bake in the oven for
10 minutes until the naan is golden. Scatter over the mint and
almonds and serve immediately.

Chilli con carne meatballs

Serves 4
371 calories per serving
Takes 30 minutes
❄

500 g (1 lb 2 oz) extra lean
   beef mince
30 g sachet chilli con carne
   spice mix
1 onion, grated
calorie controlled cooking
   spray
1 green chilli, de-seeded and
   sliced
2 tablespoons tomato purée
2 x 400 g cans chopped
   tomatoes
150 ml (5 fl oz) beef stock
400 g can black beans,
   drained and rinsed
salt and freshly ground black
   pepper

To complete the fiesta, serve with 75 g (2¾ oz) of dried brown rice, cooked according to the packet instructions, ¼ x 170 g pot reduced fat guacamole and 1 tablespoon of reduced fat soured cream per person.

1 Put the beef mince, half the chilli spice mix and the onion in a large bowl. Mix together with your hands and then shape into 24 small meatballs.

2 Heat a wide deep saucepan and spray with the cooking spray. Cook the meatballs in batches for 10 minutes, turning occasionally until browned all over and almost cooked. Remove and set aside.

3 Spray the pan again with the cooking spray and add the chilli, tomato purée and remaining spice mix. Cook for 1 minute. Stir in the tomatoes and stock and bring to the boil. Simmer for 10 minutes, stirring occasionally.

4 Return the meatballs to the pan and stir in the black beans. Simmer for a further 5 minutes until the sauce is thickened and the meatballs are cooked. Check the seasoning and serve immediately.

Variation... You can replace the beef with 500 g (1 lb 2 oz) lean turkey mince instead.

Grilled gammon with a pineapple crust

Serves 4
226 calories per serving
Takes 20 minutes

4 x 125 g (4½ oz) gammon
  steaks, visible fat removed
2 canned pineapple rings,
  drained and diced
1 spring onion, chopped finely
25 g (1 oz) fresh white
  breadcrumbs
25 g (1 oz) Parmesan cheese,
  grated finely
1 teaspoon English mustard

*This combination of ingredients is delicious with
70 g (2½ oz) of peas and a grilled tomato per person.*

1 Preheat the grill to medium and cook the gammon steaks
for 4 minutes on each side.

2 Meanwhile, mix together the pineapple and spring onion
with the breadcrumbs and cheese.

3 Spread each gammon steak with a little mustard and the
pineapple crumb mixture. Return to the grill for a further
2 minutes or until the crumbs become golden and crisp.

Perfect poultry

Orange and basil chicken

Serves 8

193 calories per serving

Takes 5 minutes to prepare, 20 minutes to cook.

125 g (4½ oz) marmalade

juice of 2 oranges

juice of 2 lemons

3 tablespoons chopped fresh basil

8 x 125 g (4½ oz) skinless boneless chicken breasts

salt and freshly ground black pepper

An excellent dish for serving to a large group of people as it's so quick to prepare and easy to cook. The tangy orange sauce glazes the chicken and keeps it really moist.

1 Preheat the oven to Gas Mark 6/200°C/fan oven 180°C. Blend the marmalade with the citrus juices and basil, season and then pour over the chicken breasts in an ovenproof dish.

2 Place the dish in the oven and cook for 20 minutes, basting the chicken with the sauce halfway through. Serve on warmed plates.

Crispy Parmesan turkey with roast tomatoes

Serves 4
248 calories per serving
Takes 25 minutes

75 g (2¾ oz) fresh white or wholemeal breadcrumbs

40 g (1½ oz) Parmesan cheese, freshly grated

4 x 125 g (4½ oz) turkey breast steaks

1 egg, beaten

calorie controlled cooking spray

250 g (9 oz) cherry tomatoes, halved

½ teaspoon caster sugar

1 tablespoon fresh thyme leaves

salt and freshly ground black pepper

Serve with 150 g (5½ oz) of cooked spaghetti per person, for a classic Italian combination.

1 Preheat the oven to Gas Mark 6/200°C/fan oven 180°C and place a baking tray in the oven to heat.

2 Mix the breadcrumbs and Parmesan cheese together on a plate. Dip the turkey breast steaks in the beaten egg and then into the crumb mixture to coat.

3 Remove the baking tray from the oven and place the coated turkey steaks on it. Spray with the cooking spray and then place the tray on the top shelf of the oven to cook for 10 minutes.

4 Meanwhile, spread the cherry tomatoes out in a roasting tin, cut side up. Sprinkle with the sugar and thyme. Season and then spray lightly with the cooking spray. Add the roasting tin to the oven and cook below the turkey for 10 minutes. Serve the turkey with the tomatoes on the side

Chicken enchiladas

Serves 4
424 calories per serving
Takes 25 minutes

8 medium flour tortillas
350 g (12 oz) skinless boneless chicken breasts, cut into thin strips
1 teaspoon chilli sauce
calorie controlled cooking spray
1 red pepper, de-seeded and sliced
1 green pepper, de-seeded and sliced
1 red onion, cut into wedges
175 g (6 oz) courgettes, cut into thin sticks
2 tablespoons chopped fresh coriander
50 g (1¾ oz) half fat Cheddar cheese, grated
1 lime, cut into wedges

These tasty wraps are quick to make and fun to eat.

1 Preheat the oven to Gas Mark 6/200°C/fan oven 180°C. Wrap the flour tortillas in foil and heat them in the oven for 10 minutes.

2 Meanwhile, mix the chicken with the chilli sauce. Spray a griddle pan with the cooking spray and heat until just smoking.

3 Cook the chicken strips for 2–3 minutes, until they are sealed. Add the peppers, onion and courgettes and cook for a further 5 minutes, until they are lightly charred. Scatter over the coriander.

4 To serve, unwrap the flour tortillas and scatter a little grated cheese over each one. Top with the cooked chicken mixture and a squeeze of juice from a lime wedge. Fold the tortilla into quarters and eat while hot.

Tip... If you don't have a griddle pan, use the heaviest frying pan you have to cook the chicken.

⊙ Variation... For a vegetarian alternative, use 350 g (12 oz) Quorn fillets, cut into strips, instead of the chicken.

Warm pan fried duck with fettuccine

Serves 2
314 calories per serving
Takes 30 minutes

75 g (2¾ oz) dried fettuccine
calorie controlled cooking
    spray
2 x 125 g (4½ oz) skinless
    boneless duck breasts
1 orange
2 heads of pak choi, leaves
    separated
2 tablespoons soy sauce
salt and freshly ground black
    pepper

Duck and orange is a classic combination. Here it is served with pasta and pak choi for a modern twist.

1 Bring a large saucepan of water to the boil, add the pasta and cook according to the packet instructions. Drain and keep warm.

2 Meanwhile, heat a non stick frying pan until hot, spray with the cooking spray and pan fry the duck breasts for 10 minutes until golden on both sides and firm to the touch. Set aside for 3–4 minutes to rest and then slice thinly. The duck should be slightly pink on the inside.

3 Finely grate the zest of the orange into the pasta and then peel and segment the orange, holding it over the pasta to collect the juice. Add the orange pieces, pak choi and soy sauce to the pasta and toss together.

4 Season and return the pasta to the heat for 1–2 minutes to wilt the pak choi. Serve the sliced duck topped with the pasta.

Creamy tarragon chicken

Serves 2
337 calories per serving
Takes 30 minutes

2 teaspoons sunflower oil
300 g (10½ oz) skinless boneless chicken breasts, cut into thin strips
150 g (5½ oz) mushrooms, sliced
2 teaspoons chopped fresh tarragon or 1 teaspoon dried tarragon
3 tablespoons sherry
150 ml (5 fl oz) chicken stock
1 tablespoon cornflour
2 tablespoons half fat crème fraîche
salt and freshly ground black pepper

This is delightful served with 60 g (2 oz) of dried tagliatelle per person, cooked according to the packet instructions.

1 Heat the oil in a large, lidded, non stick frying pan and add the chicken strips. Stir fry for 5 minutes until the chicken is sealed on all sides. Add the mushrooms and tarragon and cook for a further 2 minutes.

2 Season and add the sherry and stock. Bring to the boil, cover and simmer for 10 minutes.

3 Mix the cornflour with a little cold water to make a thin paste and stir it into the sauce. Cook, stirring, until the sauce thickens a little. Remove from the heat, stir in the crème fraîche and serve immediately.

Chilli-garlic chicken and rice

Serves 4

358 calories per serving

Takes 10 minutes to prepare,
15 minutes to cook

225 g (8 oz) dried long grain
rice

1 tablespoon toasted sesame
oil, stir fry oil or vegetable
oil

350 g (12 oz) skinless
boneless chicken breasts,
cut into strips

a bunch of spring onions,
finely sliced

175 g (6 oz) mange tout or
sugar snap peas, sliced

2 tablespoons chilli-garlic
sauce

salt and freshly ground black
pepper

1 tablespoon chopped fresh
chives, to garnish

*You can buy some excellent sauces these days, which give
a quick and tasty finish to a simple dish. This one uses a
chilli sauce flavoured with garlic.*

1 Bring a saucepan of water to the boil, add the rice and
cook according to the packet instructions. It will take about
12 minutes, so start cooking the stir fry about 8 minutes before
the rice is ready.

2 Heat the oil in a wok or large non stick frying pan and add
the chicken strips. Stir fry for about 3–4 minutes and then add
the spring onions and mange tout or sugar snap peas. Stir fry
for another 2–3 minutes.

3 Add the chilli-garlic sauce and cook for 1 minute. Season
to taste.

4 Drain the rice, divide between four warmed bowls or plates
and pile the chicken and vegetable mixture on top. Garnish
with the chives and serve at once.

Tip... If you can't find chilli-garlic sauce, add a crushed
garlic clove to the stir fry and use ordinary chilli sauce
instead.

Variations... Use a combination of white and wild rice for
extra interest.

You can add extra vegetables such as peppers or
beansprouts.

Turkey breast with raspberry sauce

Serves 4
258 calories per serving
Takes 25 minutes

calorie controlled cooking
   spray
4 x 150 g (5½ oz) turkey
   breast escalopes
juice of a lemon
1 onion, chopped finely
2 carrots, peeled and chopped
   finely
150 ml (5 fl oz) stock
1 tablespoon clear honey
100 g (3½ oz) cherry
   tomatoes, halved
100 g (3½ oz) fresh or frozen
   raspberries
25 g (1 oz) plain flour
2 tablespoons Worcestershire
   sauce
salt and freshly ground black
   pepper

*Raspberries sound unusual for a savoury sauce but the
tartness of the raspberries complements the escalopes in
this very quick and easy recipe. Serve in summer when
raspberries are plentiful with 200 g (7 oz) of steamed new
potatoes per person and green beans.*

1 Heat a large non stick frying pan and spray with the cooking
spray. Add the turkey escalopes, season and cook for 3 minutes
on each side until almost cooked through and golden brown.

2 Add the lemon juice, scrape up any juices stuck to the
pan and then add the onion, carrots and stock. Simmer for
4 minutes and then add the honey, tomatoes and raspberries.
Sprinkle with the flour.

3 Cook for a further 3 minutes, stirring, and then season and
add the Worcestershire sauce. Remove the turkey and put on
serving plates. Allow the sauce to continue simmering for a
few minutes and then pour over the turkey and serve.

Chicken teriyaki

Serves 4

354 calories per serving

Takes 20 minutes to prepare
+ 10 minutes marinating

450 g (1 lb) skinless boneless
   chicken breasts, cut into
   strips

3 tablespoons teriyaki sauce

calorie controlled cooking
   spray

6 spring onions, sliced

110 g (4 oz) baby corn

200 g (7 oz) green beans,
   halved

200 g (7 oz) beansprouts

3 x 150 g packets straight to
   wok medium noodles

*Teriyaki sauce gives a lovely sweet and sour tang and
you don't have to marinate for long for the flavours to be
absorbed into the chicken.*

1 Place the chicken strips in a non metallic bowl, pour over
the teriyaki sauce and leave to marinate for 10 minutes.

2 Lightly coat a wok or large non stick frying pan with the
cooking spray and heat until hot. Remove the chicken from
the dish using a slotted spoon and add to the pan, reserving
any leftover sauce. Stir fry for 3–4 minutes until the chicken
is beginning to brown.

3 Add the spring onions, baby corn and beans. Stir fry for
2–3 minutes.

4 Add the beansprouts and noodles, plus the reserved marinade,
and continue cooking for 1–2 minutes until everything is hot. If
the mixture gets too dry, add 1–2 tablespoons of water. Serve
immediately.

Chicken, courgette and pea pasta

Serves 4
349 calories per serving
Takes 15 minutes

250 g (9 oz) dried penne

2 courgettes, sliced

125 g (4½ oz) frozen petit pois

calorie controlled cooking spray

300 g (10½ oz) skinless boneless chicken breasts, cut into bite size pieces

1 large garlic clove, chopped finely

finely grated zest and juice of ½ a lemon

2 tablespoons half fat crème fraîche

salt and freshly ground black pepper

fresh basil leaves, to garnish (optional)

A fresh quick pasta that is perfect for a spring or summer evening.

1 Bring a large saucepan of water to the boil, add the pasta and cook according to the packet instructions, adding the courgettes and petit pois 1 minute before the end of the cooking time. Once cooked, drain the pasta and vegetables, reserving 4 tablespoons of the cooking liquid.

2 Meanwhile, heat a large non stick frying pan and spray with the cooking spray. Add the chicken and cook for 10 minutes, turning occasionally, and then add the garlic. Cook for another minute and stir in the lemon zest and juice, crème fraîche and reserved cooking liquid. Warm through, stirring, for 1 minute.

3 Add the cooked pasta and vegetables to the pan and toss until combined and warmed through. Season and serve garnished with the basil leaves, if using.

Creamy turkey and pepper fricassée

Serves 4
169 calories per serving
Takes 25 minutes

Strips of turkey and peppers cooked until meltingly tender and then slathered in a tasty, creamy sauce. Serve with a 225 g (8 oz) potato, baked in its skin, per person.

calorie controlled cooking spray

2 garlic cloves, sliced finely

400 g (14 oz) skinless boneless turkey breast, cut into fine strips

4 tablespoons soy sauce

1 chilli, de-seeded and sliced finely (optional)

2 red, yellow or orange peppers, de-seeded and sliced finely

1 tablespoon balsamic vinegar

2 tablespoons low fat fromage frais

a small bunch of fresh coriander or basil, chopped roughly

salt and freshly ground black pepper

1 Heat a large non stick frying pan and spray with the cooking spray. Add the garlic and stir fry for 1 minute.

2 Add the turkey to the pan with the soy sauce. Stir fry quickly until browned all over.

3 Add the chilli, if using, and peppers. Stir fry for a couple of minutes on a high heat, until the peppers are browned at the edges and just softening.

4 Sprinkle over the balsamic vinegar and then remove from the heat. Allow to cool for a couple of minutes and then add the fromage frais and herbs and stir through. Check the seasoning and serve.

Tortilla topped chicken bake

Serves 4
398 calories per serving
Takes 25 minutes

calorie controlled cooking spray
400 g (14 oz) skinless boneless chicken thighs, cubed
295 g can Mediterranean tomato soup
420 g can mixed beans in chilli sauce
40 g (1½ oz) tortilla chips
60 g (2 oz) half fat mature Cheddar cheese, grated

An absolute winner with everyone.

1 Preheat the oven to Gas Mark 4/180°C/160°C.

2 Heat a non stick pan and spray with the cooking spray. Add the chicken and cook for 5–8 minutes.

3 Add the soup and beans and mix well. Simmer for 5 minutes.

4 Place in an ovenproof dish, sprinkle with the tortilla chips and cheese and bake for 10 minutes, until the cheese has just melted.

Turkey tomato pasta

Serves 4

222 calories per serving

Takes 10 minutes to prepare,
20 minutes to cook

2 teaspoons olive oil

a bunch of spring onions,
sliced finely

1 garlic clove, crushed

1 green pepper, de-seeded and
chopped

50 g (1¾ oz) sun-dried
tomatoes in olive oil, rinsed
and sliced

400 g can chopped tomatoes

1 tablespoon dried oregano or
dried mixed Italian herbs

175 g (6 oz) dried pasta
shapes (e.g. shells)

150 g (5½ oz) turkey rashers

salt and freshly ground black
pepper

fresh oregano or basil leaves,
to garnish (optional)

*A delicious simple pasta dish that is full of the flavours of
the Mediterranean.*

1 Heat the oil in a large non stick saucepan and sauté the
spring onions and garlic for about 2 minutes, or until soft. Add
the green pepper and cook, stirring, for another 2 minutes.

2 Add the sun-dried tomatoes, chopped tomatoes and dried
herbs. Heat until bubbling and then turn the heat to low and
simmer, uncovered, for 10 minutes.

3 Meanwhile, bring a large saucepan of water to the boil, add
the pasta and cook for 8–10 minutes, or according to the packet
instructions, until just tender.

4 At the same time, preheat the grill to medium and grill the
turkey rashers for 1½ minutes on each side. Remove and cut
into small pieces.

5 Drain the pasta well and add it to the sauce with three
quarters of the chopped turkey rashers. Season to taste. Divide
between four warmed bowls and garnish with the oregano or
basil leaves, if using, and the reserved turkey pieces. Season
with black pepper and serve immediately.

Coconut chicken curry

Serves 2
505 calories per serving
Takes 25 minutes
❄

calorie controlled cooking
spray
300 g (10½ oz) skinless
boneless chicken breasts,
cut into bite size pieces
200 g (7 oz) sweet potato,
peeled and cubed
2 tablespoons Thai green
curry paste
250 ml (9 fl oz) chicken or
vegetable stock
6 tablespoons reduced fat
coconut milk
1 small red pepper, de-seeded
and sliced into strips
150 g (5½ oz) sugar snap peas
6 baby corn, halved
lengthways
3 tablespoons chopped fresh
coriander
salt and freshly ground black
pepper

Spices are a great way of adding flavour to dishes. Serve this fragrant curry with 60 g (2 oz) of dried brown rice per person, cooked according to the packet instructions.

1 Heat a wok or lidded non stick saucepan and spray with the cooking spray. Add the chicken and stir fry for 5 minutes until golden. Stir in the sweet potato and curry paste and cook, stirring, for 1 minute.

2 Pour in the stock and coconut milk and bring to the boil. Reduce the heat and simmer, covered, for 6 minutes. Add the pepper, sugar snap peas and baby corn and cook for about 5 minutes until the vegetables are tender.

3 Stir in the coriander and season to taste before serving.

Chargrilled chicken with polenta

Serves 2
744 calories per serving
Takes 30 minutes

300 g (10½ oz) skinless boneless chicken breasts, cut into strips
1 large red onion, cut into wedges
1 fennel bulb, cut into 6 wedges
1 red pepper, de-seeded and cut into 6 slices
2 courgettes, thinly sliced lengthways
4 teaspoons balsamic vinegar
calorie controlled cooking spray
2 tablespoons reduced fat mayonnaise
2 teaspoons reduced fat pesto
215 g (7¼ oz) ready-made polenta, cut into 6 slices
salt and freshly ground black pepper
a handful of fresh basil leaves, to garnish

This is a tasty filling version of the recipe on page 138–9.

1 In a bowl, mix the chicken, onion, fennel, pepper and courgettes with the balsamic vinegar. Season.

2 Preheat a griddle pan or non stick frying pan to hot. Spray the chicken and vegetables with the cooking spray and cook the chicken, onion, fennel and pepper for 8–10 minutes, turning once, until slightly charred and the chicken is cooked through. Remove from the pan, set aside and keep warm. Add the courgettes to the pan and cook for 5 minutes, turning once.

3 Meanwhile, in a bowl, mix together the mayonnaise and pesto and set aside.

4 Remove the courgettes and add to the chicken and vegetables. Spray the polenta with the cooking spray and cook in the pan for 3 minutes on each side. Serve the polenta with the chicken and vegetables, garnished with the basil and with the pesto dip on the side.

Fish and seafood

Pan fried scallops

Serves 2
207 calories per serving
Takes 25 minutes

50 g (1¾ oz) lamb's lettuce
6 large prepared scallops with corals (see Tip)
6 x 25 g (1 oz) lean unsmoked bacon rashers
calorie controlled cooking spray
2 tablespoons fish stock
1 tablespoon balsamic vinegar
salt and freshly ground black pepper (optional)

If you've never cooked scallops before, this recipe is a good place to start.

1 Arrange the lettuce on two plates. Gently cut the corals from the scallops and put four of them aside. Finely chop the remaining two with a sharp knife.

2 Using the back of a knife, gently stretch and flatten the bacon. Secure around each scallop with a cocktail stick, making sure the two flat sides are clear of the stick so that the scallops sit flat.

3 Spray a non stick frying pan with the cooking spray and heat it to medium-hot. Put the wrapped scallops into the hot pan and fry for 4 minutes. Turn them over, fry for another 2 minutes and then gently pull the cocktail sticks out of the scallops. (The bacon will now have 'set' and will stay in place.)

4 Add the whole corals to the pan, turning occasionally, and continue to cook everything for another minute or so. By now the bacon should be completely cooked through.

5 Remove the scallops and corals and place on the lettuce. Add the fish stock, balsamic vinegar and chopped corals to the pan, stir to pick up the flavours from the pan and allow to bubble for 1 minute. Taste the sauce and season if necessary. Strain the sauce through a small sieve over the scallop salad and serve immediately.

Tip... Supermarkets and fishmongers generally sell scallops out of their shells and ready to cook. The coral is the orange half-moon shape, attached to the white meat. If you can't find scallops with corals, the recipe will still be good.

Thai fishcakes with cucumber dipping sauce

Serves 4
120 calories per serving
Takes 20 minutes to prepare,
10 minutes to cook
❄ (fishcakes only)

2 tablespoons soy sauce

1 tablespoon artificial
sweetener

4 cm (1½ inches) cucumber,
diced finely

grated zest and juice of a lime

2 tablespoons chopped fresh
coriander

1 red chilli, de-seeded and
diced finely

2.5 cm (1 inch) fresh root
ginger, sliced

1 lemongrass stem, chopped
roughly

1 tablespoon Thai fish sauce

400 g (14 oz) skinless
haddock fillet, diced

1 egg white

1 tablespoon cornflour

60 g (2 oz) green beans,
trimmed and sliced thinly

calorie controlled cooking
spray

Although these fragrant little fishcakes are usually served as a starter in Thai restaurants, they make a great main course served with steamed broccoli and 60 g (2 oz) of dried rice per person, cooked according to the packet instructions.

1 Mix the soy sauce, sweetener and cucumber together with 1 tablespoon each of lime juice and chopped coriander and half the diced chilli. Set aside.

2 Place the lime zest and remaining lime juice in a food processor with the rest of the coriander and chilli, the ginger, lemongrass and fish sauce. Whizz together until finely chopped and then add the fish and pulse together until well blended but not over processed. Scrape the mixture into a bowl and stir in the egg white, cornflour and green beans until thoroughly combined.

3 Using wet hands, shape the mixture into 12 fishcakes. Heat a non stick frying pan and spray with the cooking spray. Cook the fishcakes in two batches for 2½ minutes on each side. Serve with the cucumber dipping sauce.

Tip... Using wet hands makes it easier to shape sticky mixtures without getting too messy.

Variation... You can use other boneless white fish such as coley or hoki in place of the haddock.

Haddock Kiev

Serves 4

224 calories per serving

Takes 10 minutes to prepare, 15 minutes to cook

❄ (fish only, while still raw and up to the end of step 2)

1 heaped teaspoon garlic purée

1 tablespoon finely chopped fresh curly parsley

1 tablespoon snipped fresh chives

50 g (1¾ oz) low fat spread

4 x 125 g (4½ oz) skinless haddock loins

8 x 15 g (½ oz) slices Parma ham

freshly ground black pepper

If the fish is really fresh, this can be prepared a day in advance, then all that's left to do is pop them in the oven. Serve with a 225 g (8 oz) potato each, cut into wedges and baked in its skin in a hot oven until crispy, 35 g (1¼ oz) of cooked peas and cooked asparagus spears per person.

1 Preheat the oven to Gas Mark 5/190°C/fan oven 170°C. In a small bowl, mix together the garlic purée, parsley, chives, low fat spread and freshly ground black pepper.

2 Put the haddock loins on a board and cut each in half. Spread the garlic butter over four halves. Top each with another piece of haddock, sandwiching the garlic spread.

3 Wrap each haddock sandwich with two slices of Parma ham to enclose the fish. Transfer to a baking tray and roast in the oven for 10–15 minutes until golden and cooked. Serve immediately.

Garlicky mussels gratin

Serves 2

122 calories per serving

Takes 10 minutes to prepare,
10 minutes to cook

Green lipped mussels from New Zealand are plump and juicy. You can buy them already cooked from most fish counters in the supermarket. Serve with a 50 g (1¾ oz) bread roll each.

25 g (1 oz) herb focaccia, torn roughly

2 garlic cloves, chopped finely

250 g (9 oz) half shell cooked New Zealand green lipped mussels (about 12)

2 tomatoes, de-seeded and diced finely

3 tablespoons dry white wine

calorie controlled cooking spray

1 Preheat the oven to Gas Mark 6/200°C/fan oven 180°C. Blend the focaccia and garlic in a food processor, or use a hand held blender, until it forms coarse breadcrumbs. Set aside. Arrange the mussels in a shallow ovenproof dish in a single layer, mussels facing upwards.

2 Scatter over the tomatoes and then drizzle over the white wine. Scatter over the focaccia crumbs, spray with the cooking spray and bake in the oven for 10 minutes until golden and bubbling hot.

Sardine pasta bake

Serves 4
440 calories per serving
Takes 30 minutes

275 g (9½ oz) dried pasta
   shapes (e.g. penne)
75 g (2¾ oz) frozen sweetcorn
   or canned sweetcorn,
   drained
2 x 120 g tins sardines in
   tomato sauce, mashed
   roughly
2 tablespoons tomato purée
150 g (5½ oz) chopped frozen
   spinach, defrosted
60 g (2 oz) mature Cheddar
   cheese, grated
salt and freshly ground black
   pepper

This is a great way to eat oily fish and makes a quick and easy mid week supper, since most of the ingredients come from the store cupboard.

1 Bring a large saucepan of water to the boil, add the pasta and cook according to the packet instructions. If using frozen sweetcorn, add for the final minute of cooking to defrost it. Drain, reserving 2 tablespoons of the cooking liquid.

2 Preheat the grill to medium. Return the pasta to the pan with the cooking liquid and mix in the sardines, tomato purée, spinach and canned sweetcorn, if using. Season. Heat for 1–2 minutes until hot and then spoon into an ovenproof dish. Sprinkle with the cheese and grill for 4–5 minutes until bubbling.

Tip... Try 200 g (7 oz) of canned tuna, drained, instead of the sardines.

Quick prawn pasta

Serves 4
458 calories per serving
Takes 10 minutes

350 g (12 oz) dried pasta
calorie controlled cooking
   spray
4 garlic cloves, chopped
200 g (7 oz) raw peeled tiger
   or king prawns, defrosted if
   frozen
200 g (7 oz) raw peeled
   prawns, defrosted if frozen
4 tablespoons sherry vinegar
150 g (5½ oz) half fat crème
   fraîche
25 g packet fresh parsley,
   chopped
salt and freshly ground black
   pepper

A luscious sauce made with lots of garlic and finished with a dash of half fat crème fraîche.

1 Bring a saucepan of water to the boil, add the pasta and cook according to the packet instructions.

2 Meanwhile, spray a large non stick frying pan with the cooking spray and put over a medium heat. Add the garlic and fry until turning brown. Add all the prawns, the vinegar and seasoning and stir fry for 4 minutes or until the large prawns are pink and cooked through.

3 Remove from the heat and stir in the crème fraîche and parsley.

4 Drain the pasta and toss with the prawn sauce. Check the seasoning and serve immediately.

Tuna with spring veg sauté

Serves 4
228 calories per serving
Takes 20 minutes

4 x 140 g (5 oz) tuna steaks
3 tablespoons soy sauce
juice of a lemon
1 teaspoon ground ginger
calorie controlled cooking spray
3 shallots, diced
150 g (5½ oz) green beans, trimmed
100 g (3½ oz) baby carrots, peeled
50 g (1¾ oz) baby courgettes, halved lengthways
50 g (1¾ oz) cherry tomatoes
150 ml (5 fl oz) vegetable stock
salt and freshly ground black pepper

Seared tuna is quick and tasty and perfect for a special meal.

1 Place the tuna steaks in a non metallic bowl. Mix together the soy sauce, lemon juice and ground ginger and pour this over the tuna steaks. Season with black pepper, cover and leave to marinate for 10–15 minutes.

2 Meanwhile, heat a wok or large frying pan, spray with the cooking spray and add the vegetables, except the cherry tomatoes. Stir fry for 5–6 minutes until they start to brown in places.

3 Add the tomatoes and pour in the vegetable stock. Turn up the heat so that the stock is bubbling well, season and cook for 6–8 minutes, stirring occasionally.

4 Meanwhile, heat a griddle pan or non stick frying pan, spray with the cooking spray and cook the drained tuna for 5–6 minutes on each side, depending on how well cooked you like your fish.

5 Serve the tuna steaks on a bed of the vegetables with a little of the sauce poured over the top.

Autumn rosti with smoked trout

Serves 2
285 calories per serving
Takes 30 minutes
✷ (rosti only)

150 g (5½ oz) sweet potato,
  peeled and halved
200 g (7 oz) swede, peeled and
  halved
175 g (6 oz) parsnips, peeled
  and halved
2 tablespoons finely chopped
  fresh flat leaf parsley
calorie controlled cooking
  spray
3 tablespoons 0% fat Greek
  yogurt
2 teaspoons grated
  horseradish from a jar or
  horseradish sauce
120 g packet smoked rainbow
  trout
salt and freshly ground black
  pepper

Serve with a simple watercress salad and lemon wedges on the side.

1 Bring a large lidded saucepan of water to the boil, add the potato and swede, bring back to the boil, cover and simmer for 5 minutes. Add the parsnips, cover again and simmer for a further 5 minutes. Drain and leave to cool slightly.

2 When cool enough to handle, coarsely grate the sweet potato, swede and parsnips into a bowl. Add the parsley and seasoning and mix together. With wet hands, shape into six small patties.

3 Heat a non stick frying pan and spray the rostis with the cooking spray. Gently cook for 8–10 minutes, turning until cooked and golden. Meanwhile, mix together the yogurt and horseradish and season. Serve the rostis topped with the smoked trout and horseradish mixture. Serve immediately.

❂ **Variation...** For a wonderful vegetarian option, see the recipe on page 133.

Stir fried monkfish with lime

Serves 1
556 calories per serving
Takes 20 minutes

75 g (2¾ oz) dried egg noodles
calorie controlled cooking
   spray
1 garlic clove, sliced thinly
2 spring onions, shredded
   finely
1 cm (½ inch) fresh
   root ginger, sliced into
   matchsticks
grated zest and juice of a lime
2 tablespoons soy sauce
100 g (3½ oz) monkfish tail,
   central bone removed and
   flesh sliced thinly
75 g (2¾ oz) mange tout,
   sliced finely
50 g (1¾ oz) baby corn
1 carrot, peeled and sliced into
   fine matchsticks
½ red pepper, de-seeded and
   sliced finely
2 baby courgettes, sliced
   finely

A very satisfying and speedy meal, with the deliciously tangy flavours of lime, garlic and fresh ginger.

1 Bring a saucepan of water to the boil, add the noodles and cook according to the packet instructions.

2 Meanwhile, heat a wok or large non stick frying pan, spray with the cooking spray and add the garlic, spring onions and ginger. Stir fry over a high heat for 1–2 minutes. Add all the other ingredients and cook for a further 3–4 minutes or until the fish is just opaque and cooked through.

3 Drain the noodles thoroughly, pile on to a plate and place the fish on top. Serve at once.

Spanish style garlic prawns

Serves 1
257 calories per serving
Takes 10 minutes

a pinch of saffron threads
50 ml (2 fl oz) dry or medium sherry
1 teaspoon olive oil
1 yellow pepper, de-seeded and sliced
1 garlic clove, sliced
½ red chilli, de-seeded and sliced
230 g can chopped tomatoes
100 g (3½ oz) raw peeled tiger prawns, defrosted if frozen
1 tablespoon chopped fresh flat leaf parsley (optional)
freshly ground black pepper

A super speedy recipe that's ideal for supper after work, or after a visit to the gym when you are hungry and want a hot filling meal in a hurry. Serve with 60 g (2 oz) of dried brown rice, cooked according to the packet instructions.

1 Crumble the saffron threads into the sherry and set aside until ready to use.

2 Heat the oil in a non stick frying pan, add the pepper and fry for 2 minutes. Stir in the garlic and chilli and fry for 30 seconds or until the garlic is golden.

3 Add the tomatoes, prawns and sherry mixture to the pan and stir fry for 2–3 minutes or until the prawns are pink and firm. Season with freshly ground black pepper and scatter with the parsley, if using, before serving.

Tips... Sherry gives this dish an authentically Spanish flavour, but if you don't like using alcohol, use vegetable stock instead.

If using frozen prawns, remember to take them out of the freezer before you leave the house in the morning, then you can have a meal ready within minutes of getting home. Spread them out on a plate, cover and leave to defrost in the fridge.

Danish cod casserole

Serves 4

206 calories per serving

Takes 10 minutes to prepare, 20 minutes to cook

calorie controlled cooking spray

1 onion, chopped finely

1 leek, sliced thickly

1 teaspoon fennel seeds, crushed lightly

2 courgettes, grated coarsely

250 g (9 oz) potatoes, peeled and cubed

150 ml (5 fl oz) skimmed milk

300 ml (10 fl oz) fish stock

400 g (14 oz) cod loin fillets, cut into large chunks

2 tomatoes, de-seeded and diced

1 tablespoon finely chopped fresh curly parsley

grated zest of ¼ orange

salt and freshly ground black pepper

A fresh tasting and flavourful fish stew.

1 Heat a lidded non stick saucepan and spray with the cooking spray. Add the onion, leek and fennel seeds and cook for 5 minutes until softened but not coloured.

2 Add the courgettes, potatoes, milk and fish stock and bring to the boil. Cover and simmer gently for 15 minutes until the potatoes are tender. Stir in the cod and simmer for 5 minutes until cooked.

3 Meanwhile, mix together the tomatoes, parsley and orange zest. Check the seasoning of the stew and serve in warmed bowls, topped with the diced tomato mixture.

Variation... This also works really well with chunks of monkfish.

Simply vegetarian

Huevos rancheros

Serves 4
292 calories per serving
Takes 25 minutes
Ⓥ
❄ (sauce only)

calorie controlled cooking
  spray
1 large onion, chopped
1 green pepper, de-seeded and
  sliced
1 large garlic clove, chopped
2 teaspoons ground cumin
½ teaspoon ground chilli
  (optional)
2 teaspoons dried oregano
2 x 400 g cans chopped
  tomatoes
200 g can kidney beans,
  drained and rinsed
4 soft wholemeal tortillas
4 eggs
salt and freshly ground black
  pepper

This Tex-Mex dish is traditionally served for breakfast but it makes a great simple supper with a large green salad.

1 Preheat the oven to Gas Mark 6/200°C/fan oven 180°C. Heat a large non stick saucepan and spray with the cooking spray. Add the onion and cook for 5 minutes, stirring regularly.

2 Spray with more cooking spray, add the pepper and cook for another 3 minutes. Stir in the garlic and cook for a further minute.

3 Add the cumin, chilli (if using), oregano, tomatoes and kidney beans to the pan and then bring up to the boil. Reduce the heat and simmer for 10–15 minutes until reduced and thickened. Season.

4 Wrap the tortillas in foil and warm through in the oven for 2–3 minutes. Meanwhile, heat a large non stick frying pan and spray with the cooking spray. Break all the eggs into the pan and fry until cooked. Serve each warm tortilla with a quarter of the sauce and a fried egg.

Courgette and Feta fritters

Serves 4 (makes 12 fritters)
186 calories per serving
Takes 15 minutes to prepare,
  15 minutes to cook.

75 g (2¾ oz) plain flour
1 egg
4 tablespoons skimmed milk
**450 g (1 lb) courgettes, grated
  coarsely**
75 g (2¾ oz) Feta, crumbled
**calorie controlled cooking
  spray**

For the salad
**½ cucumber, cut into chunky
  pieces**
4 tomatoes, chopped roughly
½ red onion, sliced thinly
**2 teaspoons chopped fresh
  mint**
**salt and freshly ground black
  pepper**

*These melting cheese fritters evoke the feeling of a Greek
island holiday. Just the thing for a light summery meal, or
serve with 60 g (2 oz) of dried rice, cooked according to
the packet instructions.*

1 Sift the flour into a bowl and beat in the egg and milk to
form a thick batter. Season. Squeeze the excess moisture
from the courgettes and then stir them into the batter, along
with the Feta.

2 Lightly coat a non stick frying pan with the cooking spray.
Cook the fritters in two batches. Ladle six heaped spoonfuls
into the frying pan and fry for 3–4 minutes on each side over
a medium heat, until golden, crisp and cooked through. Keep
warm while you cook the other six.

3 While the fritters are cooking, simply mix the salad ingredients
together, season and set aside until ready to serve with the hot
courgette and Feta fritters. Serve three fritters per person.

Cajun chick peas

Serves 2

432 calories per serving

Takes 5 minutes to prepare,
25 minutes to cook

**calorie controlled cooking
spray**

1 onion, chopped

**200 g (7 oz) butternut squash,
peeled, de-seeded and cut
into small cubes**

2 teaspoons Cajun spice

**500 g (1 lb 2 oz) passata with
garlic**

**400 g can chick peas, drained
and rinsed**

2 x 60 g (2 oz) pitta breads

*Cajun spice is a mixture of spices, including chilli, used a
lot in New Orleans cooking. Try it dusted on a lamb chop
or a skinless chicken breast before grilling.*

1 Spray a non stick pan with the cooking spray and heat until
hot. Add the onion and squash and stir fry for 5 minutes, adding
a splash of water if they start to stick. Add the spice and cook
for a further minute.

2 Stir in the passata and then the chick peas. Bring to the boil,
reduce the heat to a simmer and cook for 25 minutes until the
squash is tender and the mixture has thickened.

3 Meanwhile, preheat the grill to medium and toast the pitta
breads on both sides for a minute or so until hot. Cut into strips
and serve with a bowl of the chick peas.

Tip... You can freeze any excess passata for up to 3 months.

Variation... Make this with a 410 g can of butter beans,
drained and rinsed, instead of the chick peas.

Stir fried vegetables with black bean sauce

Serves 4

75 calories per serving

Takes 15 minutes to prepare,
15 minutes to cook

**calorie controlled cooking
spray**
1 onion, sliced
2 garlic cloves, crushed
2 cm (¾ inch) fresh root
ginger, chopped
300 g (10½ oz) vegetables
(e.g. courgettes, broccoli, red
pepper), sliced thinly
1 yellow pepper, de-seeded
and sliced
150 g (5½ oz) green beans,
trimmed and cut in half
4 tablespoons black bean
sauce

*This is a wonderfully colourful version of the recipe on
page 54.*

1 Heat a wok or large non stick frying pan and spray with the
cooking spray. Add the onion, garlic and ginger to the wok or
pan and stir fry for 4–5 minutes.

2 Add all the vegetables, including the yellow pepper and green
beans, and stir fry for another 2–3 minutes.

3 Add the black bean sauce and 100 ml (3½ fl oz) of water to
the wok or pan and stir fry for another 5–6 minutes, until the
sauce has thickened.

Tip... For stir frying, always make sure your wok or frying
pan is quite hot before adding the first ingredient.

Spinach gnocchi gratin

Serves 4

329 calories per serving

Takes 10 minutes to prepare,
20 minutes to cook

500 g packet fresh gnocchi

150 g (5½ oz) frozen chopped
spinach, defrosted

2 garlic cloves, crushed

250 g (9 oz) reduced fat onion
and chive cottage cheese

2 egg yolks

50 g (1¾ oz) mild or hot
piquante peppers, sliced
finely

15 g (½ oz) pine nut kernels,
toasted

freshly ground black pepper

*A dish that even meat-lovers will enjoy. Serve with a
35 g (1¼ oz) slice of garlic bread per person and a large
green salad.*

1 Preheat the oven to Gas Mark 4/180°C/fan oven 160°C.
Bring a large saucepan of water to the boil, add the gnocchi
and cook for 2 minutes. Drain and return to the pan.

2 Meanwhile, squeeze the excess water from the spinach and
put into a large bowl. Stir in the garlic, cottage cheese, egg
yolks and peppers and lots of freshly ground black pepper. Stir
into the gnocchi to coat and then spoon into a 1.2 litre (2 pint)
ovenproof dish.

3 Heat a small non stick frying pan and dry fry the pine nut
kernels until golden, Be careful not to let them burn. Sprinkle
the pine nut kernels over the gnocchi and bake in the oven for
20 minutes until golden.

Hoisin Quorn and broccoli stir fry

Serves 4
336 calories per serving
Takes 20 minutes

200 g (7 oz) broccoli, broken into florets
calorie controlled cooking spray
125 g (4½ oz) mange tout
6 spring onions, sliced diagonally
2 large garlic cloves, sliced thinly
4 cm (1½ inch) fresh root ginger, grated
200 g (7 oz) dried thick rice noodles
250 g (9 oz) Quorn mince
6 tablespoons hoisin sauce
3 tablespoons soy sauce
1 teaspoon toasted sesame oil
a large handful of beansprouts
2 tablespoons chopped fresh coriander, to garnish

Quick, easy and nutritious, stir fries tick all the right boxes when it comes to creating a satisfying meal in minutes. If you wish, add a sprinkling of fresh chilli for an extra kick.

1 Bring a saucepan of water to the boil, add the broccoli and cook for 2 minutes. Cool under cold running water and drain well.

2 Heat a wok or large non stick frying pan and spray with the cooking spray. Add the mange tout, broccoli, half the spring onions, the garlic and ginger and stir fry for 2 minutes, adding a splash of water if necessary to prevent them from sticking.

3 Meanwhile, bring another saucepan of water to the boil, add the rice noodles and cook according to the packet instructions. Drain.

4 Spray the vegetables with the cooking spray and add the Quorn mince. Stir fry to break up any lumps and heat through. Pour in the hoisin sauce, soy sauce, sesame oil and 6 tablespoons of water. Stir fry for a further 2 minutes before adding the beansprouts.

5 Serve the mince mixture with the noodles and sprinkled with the reserved spring onions and the coriander.

Spring vegetable stew

Serves 4
218 calories per serving
Takes 2 minutes to prepare,
 20 minutes to cook

400 g (14 oz) new potatoes,
 scrubbed
600 ml (20 fl oz) hot vegetable
 stock
40 g (1½ oz) pesto sauce
a bunch of spring onions,
 chopped roughly
2 garlic cloves, sliced into
 slivers
200 g (7 oz) sugar snap peas
200 g (7 oz) runner beans, cut
 diagonally
200 g (7 oz) baby carrots,
 scrubbed and halved or
 quartered lengthways
100 g (3½ oz) frozen petit pois
100 g (3½ oz) frozen shelled
 broad beans
a bunch of fresh basil or mint,
 chopped, to serve

A fresh-tasting spring stew full of cheerful colours and goodness.

1 Put the potatoes in a saucepan, pour the hot stock over, bring to the boil and cook for 15–20 minutes until just tender.

2 Add the pesto sauce and the rest of the vegetables. Cook for another 5 minutes and then serve sprinkled with the basil or mint.

Tips... Pesto sauce is available in jars from the pasta sauce section of supermarkets or it can be bought from the chilled sauces or delicatessan.

Pesto is also good on baked potatoes instead of butter or cheese; spread it sparingly over fish and then grill, or swirl into soup instead of fresh herbs.

Variation... Use red pepper purée, 1 tablespoon of hot harissa paste or tapenade instead of the pesto.

Autumn rosti with chargrilled vegetables

Serves 2
285 calories per serving
Takes 30 minutes
❄ (rosti only)

150 g (5½ oz) sweet potato,
   peeled and halved
200 g (7 oz) swede, peeled and
   halved
175 g (6 oz) parsnips, peeled
   and halved
2 tablespoons finely chopped
   fresh flat leaf parsley
calorie controlled cooking
   spray
1 red or yellow pepper,
   de-seeded and sliced
1 courgette, sliced
50 g (1¾ oz) light halloumi,
   sliced
3 tablespoons 0% fat Greek
   yogurt
2 teaspoons grated
   horseradish from a jar or
   horseradish sauce
salt and freshly ground black
   pepper

This is a fantastic vegetarian version of the recipe on *page 113.*

1 Bring a large lidded saucepan of water to the boil, add the potato and swede, bring back to the boil, cover and simmer for 5 minutes. Add the parsnips, cover again and simmer for a further 5 minutes. Drain and leave to cool slightly.

2 When cool enough to handle, coarsely grate the sweet potato, swede and parsnips into a bowl. Add the parsley and seasoning and mix together. With wet hands, shape into six small patties. Preheat the grill to medium-high.

3 Heat a non stick frying pan and spray the rostis with the cooking spray. Gently cook for 8–10 minutes, turning until cooked and golden.

4 Meanwhile, line the grill pan with foil and place the pepper and courgette slices on the grill tray. Spray with the cooking spray and grill for 3–4 minutes on each side or until the vegetables are slightly charred. Remove to a plate, place the halloumi slices on the grill tray and grill for 2–3 minutes until browned.

5 Mix together the yogurt and horseradish and season. Serve the rostis topped with the horseradish mixture, chargrilled vegetables and halloumi slices.

Ratatouille baked eggs

Serves 4
134 calories per serving
Takes 30 minutes

1 red onion, diced
2 courgettes, diced
2 red peppers, de-seeded
    and diced
150 g (5½ oz) chestnut
    mushrooms
1 tablespoon dried herbes
    de Provence
calorie controlled cooking
    spray
150 g (5½ oz) cherry
    tomatoes, halved
4 eggs
salt and freshly ground black
    pepper

Serve with 150 g (5½ oz) mashed potato made with
2 tablespoons of skimmed milk per person, shaped into
small patties and sautéed in calorie controlled cooking
spray until golden.

1 Preheat the oven to Gas Mark 7/220°C/fan oven 200°C.
Put the onion, courgettes, peppers and mushrooms in a
non stick roasting tin and sprinkle over the dried herbs and
seasoning. Spray with the cooking spray and toss to coat.
Cook in the oven for 15 minutes.

2 Stir the tomatoes into the roasting tin and cook in the oven
for a further 5 minutes.

3 Remove from the oven and make four wells between the
vegetables. Crack an egg into each well, return to the oven
and bake for a further 5–6 minutes until the eggs are just set.
Serve immediately.

Variations... This quick supper is a great way to use up
leftovers. Any vegetables will work, such as marrow or
squash – just ensure the veggies are all tender before
adding the eggs in step 3.

You can add 4 x 55 g (2 oz) low fat pork sausages, chopped,
along with the vegetables in step 1 and cook as above.

Tofu Thai curry

Serves 4
146 calories per serving
Takes 10 minutes to prepare,
  20 minutes to cook

calorie controlled cooking
   spray

2 garlic cloves, crushed

2.5 cm (1 inch) fresh root
   ginger, chopped finely

1 lemongrass stem, sliced
   finely

2 kaffir lime leaves, chopped
   finely

4 shallots or 2 small red
   onions, sliced finely

1 teaspoon Thai red curry
   paste

1 tablespoon soy sauce

175 g (6 oz) firm tofu, drained
   and cubed

600 ml (20 fl oz) vegetable
   stock

100 ml (3½ fl oz) reduced fat
   coconut milk

2 red peppers, de-seeded and
   sliced finely

1 head broccoli, cut into
   florets

1 small head cauliflower, cut
   into florets

100 g (3½ oz) button
   mushrooms, quartered

a bunch of fresh coriander or
   basil, roughly chopped, to
   garnish

*Ingredients such as coconut milk, lemongrass and kaffir
lime leaves give Thai curries their distinctive flavour.*

1 Heat a wok or large non stick frying pan and spray with
the cooking spray. Stir fry the garlic, ginger, lemongrass, lime
leaves and shallots or onions with a few tablespoons of water
until softened.

2 Add the curry paste, soy sauce and tofu. Stir gently to coat
the tofu and then add all the other ingredients except the
garnish. Cook gently (do not boil) for 15 minutes, or until the
broccoli and cauliflower are just tender.

3 Scatter with the coriander or basil and serve.

Tip... Instead of the kaffir lime leaves, you can use the
grated zest and juice of a lime, added at the end with
the coriander.

Chargrilled vegetables with polenta

Serves 2
522 calories per serving
Takes 25 minutes

- 1 large red onion, cut into wedges
- 1 fennel bulb, cut into 6 wedges
- 1 red pepper, de-seeded and cut into 6 slices
- 2 courgettes, thinly sliced lengthways
- 4 teaspoons balsamic vinegar
- calorie controlled cooking spray
- 2 tablespoons reduced fat mayonnaise
- 2 teaspoons reduced fat pesto
- 215 g (7¼ oz) ready-made polenta, cut into 6 slices
- salt and freshly ground black pepper
- a handful of fresh basil leaves, to garnish

You can find ready made polenta in large supermarkets, sold in a block. Serve with 15 g (½ oz) of grated Parmesan cheese per person.

1 In a bowl, mix the onion, fennel, pepper and courgettes with the balsamic vinegar. Season.

2 Preheat a griddle pan or non stick frying pan to hot. Spray the vegetables with the cooking spray and cook the onion, fennel and pepper for 8 minutes, turning once, until slightly charred. Remove the vegetables, set aside and keep warm. Add the courgettes to the pan and cook for 5 minutes, turning once.

3 Meanwhile, in a bowl, mix together the mayonnaise and pesto and set aside.

4 Remove the courgettes and add to the other vegetables. Spray the polenta with the cooking spray and cook in the pan for 3 minutes on each side. Serve the polenta with the vegetables, garnished with the basil and with the pesto dip on the side.

Variation... For a meaty version, see the recipe on page 97.

Watercress and blue cheese pasta

Serves 4
385 calories per serving
Takes 15 minutes
Ⓥ

350 g (12 oz) dried pasta
50 g (1¾ oz) Danish Blue cheese
100 g (3½ oz) low fat soft cheese
4 tablespoons skimmed milk
175 g (6 oz) watercress, chopped roughly
salt and freshly ground black pepper

This recipe uses a little strong flavoured Danish Blue cheese to create plenty of flavour.

1 Bring a saucepan of water to the boil, add the pasta and cook according to the packet instructions. Drain.

2 Meanwhile, put the cheeses and milk in a large pan and heat, stirring gently, until they are melted and combined smoothly.

3 Toss the pasta with the sauce and watercress and season. Serve immediately.

Stir fried cauliflower and cashews

Serves 4

297 calories per serving

Takes 10 minutes to prepare, 15 minutes to cook

calorie controlled cooking spray

2 garlic cloves, sliced finely

2.5 cm (1 inch) fresh root ginger, finely chopped

1 red onion, sliced finely

100 g (3½ oz) cashew nuts

1 large cauliflower, broken into bite-sized florets

2 large carrots, peeled and sliced into thin rounds

200 ml (7 fl oz) passata

½ teaspoon dried chilli flakes or 1 fresh chilli, de-seeded and finely chopped (optional)

2 tablespoons low fat natural yogurt

salt and freshly ground black pepper

a large bunch of fresh coriander, chopped, to serve (optional)

Serve with 60 g (2 oz) of dried brown rice per person, cooked according to the packet instructions.

1 Spray a wok or large, lidded, non stick frying pan with the cooking spray, add the garlic, ginger, onion and cashew nuts and stir fry for a few minutes until golden.

2 Add the cauliflower, carrots, passata, chilli, if using, and 100 ml (3½ fl oz) of water. Stir, cover and simmer for 10 minutes, or until the cauliflower and carrots are just tender.

3 Remove from the heat, allow to cool a little and then season to taste and stir through the yogurt. Sprinkle with the coriander, if using, and serve.

Squash and spinach tortilla

Serves 4
199 calories per serving
Takes 30 minutes

This dish is utterly delicious. Serve with a crisp salad of mixed leaves and cherry tomatoes with a sprinkling of balsamic vinegar. Tortillas are also good cold in picnics and lunchboxes.

800 g (1 lb 11 oz) butternut squash, peeled, de-seeded and diced finely

6 eggs

150 ml (5 fl oz) skimmed milk

1 teaspoon Dijon mustard

calorie controlled cooking spray

150 g (5½ oz) baby spinach leaves, washed

salt and freshly ground black pepper

1 Bring a large saucepan of water to the boil, add the squash and cook for 10–15 minutes, until tender. Drain.

2 Meanwhile, in a large bowl, beat together the eggs, milk and mustard and season.

3 Heat a large (20 cm/8 inch) non stick frying pan and spray with the cooking spray. Add the squash and stir fry for a few minutes, until it turns golden. Add the spinach and stir fry for a further few minutes, until wilted. Tip the egg mixture into the pan.

4 Stir gently together and then cook over the lowest heat, without stirring, for 10–12 minutes or until the bottom is golden and the tortilla is nearly set. Preheat the grill to medium.

5 Slide the pan under the preheated grill for a few minutes, until the top is golden and puffy and the egg is completely set. Cut into four wedges and serve.

Tip... It is necessary to keep the heat very low so that the bottom of the tortilla does not burn before it is cooked through

Risotto verde

Serves 4
299 calories per serving
Takes 30 minutes

**calorie controlled cooking
  spray**
**300 g (10½ oz) dried risotto
  rice**
**150 g (5½ oz) green beans,
  trimmed and cut into 5 cm
  (2 inch) lengths**
**1.2 litres (2 pints) hot
  vegetable stock**
**150 g (5½ oz) chopped frozen
  spinach**
**2 tablespoons chopped fresh
  parsley**
**1 tablespoon chopped fresh
  dill**
**finely grated zest and juice of
  a lemon**

*Green and gorgeous, this creamy risotto is full of lovely
herbs and fresh green vegetables.*

1 Spray a large non stick frying pan with the cooking spray
and heat until hot. Add the rice and beans and cook, stirring
for 1 minute until the rice is opaque. Add a ladleful of stock,
let it bubble and be absorbed before adding more, a little at a
time. Stir occasionally until all the stock is used and the rice is
tender.

2 Stir in the spinach and, once defrosted, add the herbs. Warm
over a gentle heat until hot and then add the lemon zest and
juice. Serve in warmed bowls.

Variation... You can use the same amount of broccoli, instead
of beans, but you will need to steam the florets in step 1
and add to the risotto at the last minute in step 2.

Chick pea and vegetable curry

Serves 6
196 calories per serving
Takes 30 minutes.

400 g (14 oz) potatoes, peeled
and diced

2 large carrots, peeled and
diced

250 g (9 oz) cauliflower,
broken into florets

150 g (5½ oz) green beans,
trimmed and halved

calorie controlled cooking
spray

1 onion, chopped

2 tablespoons curry paste

400 g can chopped tomatoes

150 g (5½ oz) low fat natural
yogurt

410 g can chick peas, drained
and rinsed

2 tablespoons chopped fresh
coriander, to garnish

A great panful of curry for feeding a crowd; the chick peas really take on the spicy flavours of the sauce. Serve with 60 g (2 oz) of dried rice, cooked according to the packet instructions. Any leftovers taste even better the next day.

1 Bring a large saucepan of water to the boil, add the potatoes and carrots and cook for 5 minutes. Add the cauliflower and green beans, cook for another 5 minutes and then drain the vegetables.

2 Meanwhile, heat a large non stick pan, spray with the cooking spray and brown the onion, adding a splash of water if it starts to stick. Stir in the curry paste, cook for 1 minute and then add the tomatoes and yogurt.

3 Mix the vegetables and chick peas into the curry sauce and cook for 10 minutes. Serve topped with the chopped coriander.

Mushroom and spinach towers

Serves 2

131 calories per serving

Takes 30 minutes

4 large flat mushrooms

calorie controlled cooking spray

1 leek, chopped finely

2 garlic cloves, chopped finely

200 g (7 oz) canned cannellini beans, drained and rinsed

1 teaspoon dried thyme

grated zest of a small lemon and 2 tablespoons lemon juice

a few drops of Tabasco sauce

175 g (6 oz) baby spinach leaves, washed

salt and freshly ground black pepper

2 teaspoons balsamic vinegar, to serve (optional)

This is so simple to make but bursting with flavour.

1 Preheat the oven to Gas Mark 6/200°C/fan oven 180°C. Place the mushrooms on a piece of foil large enough to make a parcel. Spray with the cooking spray and add 2 teaspoons of water. Season and fold the foil to enclose the mushrooms. Place on a baking tray and bake for 20 minutes or until tender.

2 Meanwhile, spray a non stick saucepan with the cooking spray and fry the leek for 3 minutes until tender, adding a splash of water if it starts to stick. Add the garlic, cannellini beans, thyme, lemon zest, lemon juice and Tabasco sauce and cook for 2 minutes, adding a little more water if necessary. Season well and transfer the mixture to a food processor, or use a hand held blender. Whizz until puréed and keep warm.

3 Meanwhile, bring a saucepan of water to the boil and steam the spinach for 2 minutes until wilted. Drain well to remove any excess water.

4 To serve, put one mushroom on each serving plate. Divide the bean purée between the mushrooms and top with the spinach and then another mushroom. Season and drizzle with the balsamic vinegar, if using.

Desserts and bakes

Chocolate mousse with raspberries

Serves 4
227 calories per serving
Takes 25 minutes + chilling

❄

75 g (2¾ oz) plain chocolate
   (minimum 70% cocoa
   solids), broken into pieces
1 tablespoon unsweetened
   cocoa powder
1 tablespoon caster sugar
2 eggs, separated
4 tablespoons whipping cream

To serve
100 g (3½ oz) raspberries
fresh mint leaves
1 teaspoon icing sugar
   (optional)

Velvet smooth and very chocolatey – this is a dream dessert.

1 Bring a saucepan of water to a simmer, place the chocolate in a bowl and position over the gently simmering water to melt.

2 Meanwhile, dissolve the cocoa powder and sugar in 3 tablespoons of hot water. Remove the bowl of chocolate from the heat and add the cocoa mixture, stirring until smooth and blended. Beat the egg yolks and stir into the chocolate mixture.

3 Whip the cream in a chilled bowl until it holds its shape. Keep it cool in the fridge.

4 In a clean, grease-free bowl, whisk the egg whites until they form stiff peaks. With a metal spoon, fold them through the chocolate mixture together with the whipped cream. Divide the mixture between four small serving glasses or ramekins. Chill the desserts until ready to serve.

5 Decorate with the raspberries, mint leaves and a dusting of icing sugar, if using.

Tip... To prevent a skin from forming on the surface of the chocolate mixture as it cools down, cover with a circle of dampened greaseproof paper.

Variation... Top the chocolate mousse with a mixture of soft summer fruits, if you prefer – strawberries and blueberries would be lovely.

Pear strudels

Serves 2
125 calories per serving
Takes 30 minutes

4 x 15 g (½ oz) filo pastry
   sheets, measuring
   30 x 40 cm (12 x 16 inches),
   defrosted if frozen
calorie controlled cooking
   spray
1 ripe, but not mushy pear,
   peeled, halved and core
   scooped out with a teaspoon
½ teaspoon ground cinnamon
2 teaspoons maple syrup

These are extremely easy to make with most of the time taken up with baking so you can sit and relax. Serve with a 60 g (2 oz) scoop of low fat vanilla ice cream per person.

1 Preheat the oven to Gas Mark 6/200°C/fan oven 180°C. Take one sheet of pastry and spray one half with the cooking spray. Fold in half and spray again. Place another sheet on top, spray one half and fold over. You should have an 18 x 15 cm (7 x 6 inch) rectangle. Spray with the cooking spray.

2 Put a pear half in the centre of the pastry rectangle and sprinkle with half the cinnamon. Gather up the pastry around the pear and scrunch it to make a little tart. Spray with the cooking spray and repeat the process to make a second strudel.

3 Spray a baking tray with the cooking spray, place the strudels on the tray and bake for 20 minutes until golden. Leave to cool slightly and drizzle with the maple syrup before serving.

Syrup sponges

Serves 2
237 calories per serving
Takes 30 minutes

❄

calorie controlled cooking spray
40 g (1½ oz) low fat spread
25 g (1 oz) light brown soft sugar
2 egg whites, beaten
50 g (1¾ oz) self raising flour, sifted
2 teaspoons golden syrup

Sponge puddings needn't be heavy and stodgy, as this tasty pudding proves.

1 Preheat the oven to Gas Mark 5/190°C/fan oven 170°C. Lightly spray two ovenproof 150 ml (5 fl oz) pudding basins or ramekins with the cooking spray.

2 Whisk together the low fat spread and sugar until pale and creamy. Gradually add the egg whites, whisking until well combined each time. Carefully fold in the flour.

3 Mix the golden syrup with 2 tablespoons of hot water and spoon into the base of the pudding basins or ramekins. Top with the cake mixture and bake for 15–20 minutes until golden and risen. Cool slightly before turning out to serve.

Fruity meringue

Serves 4
131 calories per serving
Takes 25 minutes

100 g (3½ oz) blackberries
100 g (3½ oz) blackcurrants
  or redcurrants
100 g (3½ oz) blueberries
150 g (5½ oz) raspberries
150 g (5½ oz) strawberries,
  hulled
50 g (1¾ oz) black grapes,
  de-seeded if necessary
artificial sweetener, to taste
3 egg whites
3 tablespoons caster sugar
4 tablespoons single cream,
  to serve

This is a perfect recipe for late summer when fresh fruit is at its best.

1 Preheat the oven to Gas Mark 4/180°C/fan oven 160°C.

2 Prepare all the fruit, cutting any large strawberries in half. Put them all into a large ovenproof baking dish with 2 tablespoons of cold water and bake for about 5–6 minutes, until the juice starts to run. Remove from the oven and sweeten to taste with artificial sweetener.

3 In a clean, grease-free bowl, whisk the egg whites until stiff peaks form. Whisk in the sugar. Pile the meringue on top of the fruit and bake for about 5–6 minutes until golden brown.

4 Serve while warm, with 1 tablespoon of single cream per portion.

Variation... If you can't find all the different types of fruit, make substitutions. For example, use cherries instead of blackberries, or just use more of the varieties you have.

Strawberry pancakes

Serves 4

172 calories per serving

Takes 15 minutes to prepare,
15 minutes to cook

❄ (pancakes only)

1 egg
100 g (3½ oz) plain flour
a pinch of salt
a pinch of ground cinnamon
300 ml (10 fl oz) skimmed milk
calorie controlled cooking
spray
1 teaspoon icing sugar

For the filling

225 g (8 oz) fresh
strawberries, hulled and
sliced
2 tablespoons port
2 tablespoons reduced sugar
strawberry jam

*Pancakes are not just for Pancake Day – try this delightful
summery recipe for a change from the usual type of
dessert.*

1 Place the egg, flour, salt, cinnamon and milk in a blender,
or use a hand held blender, and whizz until smooth.

2 Heat a heavy based, non stick, 20 cm (8 inch) frying pan
until just smoking and spray the pan with the cooking spray.
Drizzle a little of the batter on to the base of the pan, swirling
to give a thin even coating. Cook for 1 minute and then flip over
and cook for a further minute. Continue until all the batter has
been used, stacking the cooked pancakes on to a plate sitting
over a pan of gently simmering water.

3 Place the strawberries in a pan with the port and jam and
heat gently until the jam melts and coats the strawberries with
a thin syrup.

4 Serve two pancakes each, filled with a little of the
strawberry mixture and dusted lightly with a little icing sugar.
Serve at once.

Tip... Pancakes can be frozen in single serve batches. Heat
them through in a non stick pan and fill with sliced fresh
fruit for a speedy snack.

Rhubarb fool with crunchy oat topping

Serves 4
145 calories per serving
Takes 20 minutes

100 g (3½ oz) porridge oats
24 g sachet raspberry sugar free jelly
200 ml (7 fl oz) boiling water
450 g (1 lb) rhubarb, chopped
200 g (7 oz) 0% fat Greek yogurt
4 tablespoons artificial sweetener

The tart flavour of rhubarb is bought out by this lovely pink fool.

1 Preheat the oven to Gas Mark 4/180°C/fan oven 160°C. Place the oats on a baking tray and bake for about 10 minutes until golden.

2 Meanwhile, place the jelly and boiling water in a medium saucepan. Bring to the boil, stirring until the jelly has dissolved. Add the rhubarb and then cover and simmer for 10 minutes until the rhubarb is tender.

3 Using a food processor, or a hand held blender, purée the rhubarb and jelly mixture and then allow to cool for 15 minutes. Add the yogurt and sweetener and pulse to blend it all together.

4 Pour into one large serving bowl or four individual glasses. Sprinkle over the oats to serve. Serve warm or leave to chill and set in the fridge.

Coffee custards

Serves 4

109 calories per serving

Takes 10 minutes to prepare,
  15 minutes to cook

300 ml (10 fl oz) skimmed milk
2 eggs plus 2 yolks, beaten
40 g (1½ oz) low fat soft
  cheese
2 tablespoons instant coffee
2 tablespoons artificial
  sweetener
a kettleful of boiling water

These luxurious baked custards can be enjoyed warm or chilled depending on your mood – and the weather.

1 Preheat the oven to Gas Mark 3/160°C/fan oven 140°C. In a non stick saucepan, bring the milk to simmering point.

2 Meanwhile, in a mixing bowl, gradually beat the whole eggs and egg yolks into the soft cheese, using a wooden spoon. Dissolve the instant coffee and sweetener in 1 tablespoon of boiling water and then add this to the egg mixture.

3 Slowly mix in the hot milk, stirring until smooth. Pour the coffee custard through a strainer (to remove any eggy threads) into four ramekins set in a roasting tin. Pour the remaining boiling water into the tin so that it comes halfway up the ramekins. Bake in the oven for 15 minutes until the custards feel fairly firm but are still slightly wobbly in the centre.

4 Carefully lift the ramekins out of the hot water. Serve warm, or cool and chill in the fridge if desired.

Apple and blackberry tarts

Serves 6
177 calories per serving
Takes 25 minutes

6 x 15 g (½ oz) filo pastry
   sheets, measuring
   30 x 40 cm (12 x 16 inches),
   defrosted if frozen
4 tablespoons light or
   delicately flavoured olive oil
350 g (12 oz) cooking apples,
   peeled, cored and sliced
1 tablespoon lemon juice
125 g (4½ oz) blackberries
artificial sweetener, to taste

To serve

4 tablespoons 0% fat Greek
   yogurt
2 teaspoons icing sugar
fresh mint or blackberry
   leaves (optional)

*Make these wonderful fruit filled tarts with filo pastry,
brushed with a delicately flavoured olive oil rather than
butter.*

1 Preheat the oven to Gas Mark 5/190°C/fan oven 170°C.

2 Unfold the filo pastry sheets and cut the pastry into six piles,
each measuring approximately 10 cm (4 inches) square. Layer
these filo squares in six individual tartlet tins, brushing each
pastry sheet with a little olive oil. Pack a little crumpled foil into
each tartlet tin and bake for 8–10 minutes until the pastry is
golden brown.

3 Meanwhile, place the apples in a saucepan with the lemon
juice and a couple of tablespoons of water and cook until
tender – about 5–6 minutes. Remove from the heat and stir in
the blackberries. Cool slightly and then sweeten to taste with
the sweetener.

4 Remove the foil from the filo pastry tarts and spoon in the
apple and blackberry filling. Top each one with a tablespoon of
Greek yogurt or serve it on the side. Sprinkle with icing sugar
and serve, decorated with the mint or blackberry leaves, if
using.

Variation... Fill the tarts with soft summer fruits – a mixture
of 175 g (6 oz) of strawberries, 175 g (6 oz) of raspberries
and 125 g (4½ oz) of blueberries would taste lovely.

Fruit-full vanilla omelette

Serves 4
209 calories per serving
Takes 15 minutes

420 g canned apricots in
natural juice
25 g (1 oz) raisins or sultanas
1 small banana, sliced
1 tablespoon cornflour
a pinch of ground cinnamon
4 eggs, separated
1 tablespoon artificial
sweetener
1 teaspoon vanilla essence
4 teaspoons low fat spread
4 teaspoons icing sugar, for
sprinkling

*Soufflé omelettes are quick, delicious and very nutritious
and they're surprisingly easy to make.*

1 Put the apricots, with their juice, into a saucepan. Add the
raisins or sultanas and banana. Blend the cornflour to a paste
with a little water and stir in. Heat gently, stirring until thickened.
Add the cinnamon and keep warm over a low heat.

2 To make the omelettes, beat the egg yolks together, adding
the sweetener and vanilla essence. In a separate, clean,
grease-free bowl, and using clean beaters, whisk the egg
whites until stiff peaks form and then fold into the egg yolks.

3 Preheat the grill to medium-high.

4 Making one omelette at a time, melt 1 teaspoon of low fat
spread in an omelette pan with a heatproof handle. Add a
quarter of the egg mixture and cook for about 2 minutes until
the base is set. Place under the grill and cook until the surface
is just firm. Set aside and keep warm while you make the
remaining omelettes.

5 Transfer the omelettes to warmed plates, spoon a quarter
of the fruit mixture on to each, fold over and serve, sprinkled
with the icing sugar.

Tip... Remember that egg whites will not whip if there is
any trace of grease in the bowl or on the beaters and that
includes the egg yolk, so be very careful when separating
them.

Cheese and celery scones

Makes 12
191 calories per serving
Takes 25 minutes
Ⓥ
❄ (up to 1 month)

450 g (1 lb) self raising flour,
  plus 1 teaspoon for rolling
1 teaspoon salt
2 teaspoons baking powder
75 g (2¾ oz) low fat spread
150 g (5½ oz) half fat Cheddar
  cheese, grated
1 celery stick, diced
300 ml (10 fl oz) semi
  skimmed milk

These scones are best enjoyed straight out of the oven
with a spread of low fat cream cheese. Alternatively, keep
them in an airtight container for when friends pop by.

1 Preheat the oven to Gas Mark 7/220°C/fan oven 200°C.

2 Sift the flour, salt and baking powder into a large bowl. Using your fingertips, rub the low fat spread into the flour mixture until it resembles fine breadcrumbs.

3 Stir in the grated cheese and celery. Pour in the milk and mix gently so that you have a soft loose dough – be sure not to over mix.

4 Turn out the dough on to a floured work surface and then roll it out to about 2 cm (¾ inch) thick. Cut out 12 rounds with a biscuit cutter and place them on a non stick baking tray.

5 Bake in the oven for 8–10 minutes, until golden and risen. Remove from the oven and place them on a cooling rack until cool.

Tip... These scones can be made in a food processor: place the dry ingredients in the food processor, add the low fat spread and blend for a few seconds. Stir in the cheese and celery, add the milk and blend again. Continue from step 4.

Variation... Try using 80 g (3 oz) of blue cheese with chopped cherry tomatoes or spring onions instead of the Cheddar and celery.

Lemon and vanilla fingers

Makes 12 fingers
70 calories per serving
Takes 15 minutes to prepare,
 10 minutes to cook

2 large eggs
85 g (3 oz) caster sugar
1 teaspoon vanilla extract
finely grated zest of a lemon
85 g (3 oz) plain flour, sifted

You'll find these delicious fingers very versatile.

1 Grease and line a large heavy metal baking tray with non stick baking parchment. Heat the oven to Gas Mark 6/200°C/fan oven 180°C.

2 Half fill a medium saucepan with water and bring to a gentle boil. Put the eggs, sugar and vanilla extract into a large heatproof bowl and place the bowl over the pan of water. Using an electric hand held whisk (or balloon whisk if you have to beat by hand) beat as fast as possible until you have a firm, pale golden foam – the mixture should leave a trail when you lift out the beaters.

3 Remove the bowl from the heat, continue whisking for 2–3 minutes and then gently fold in the lemon zest and flour using a large metal spoon.

4 Fit a plain 1.5 cm (⅝ inch) nozzle into a piping bag. Put the bag into a tall jug and roll down the top. Spoon the mixture into the piping bag.

5 Twist the top to seal the bag with one hand and, holding the nozzle in the other hand, pipe 12 straight lengths about 10 cm (4 inches) long on to the baking tray. If you don't own a piping bag, spoon on mounds of the mixture, flattening them with the back of a teaspoon to make 12 rounds about 3 cm (1¼ inches) in diameter.

6 Bake for 5–7 minutes until the biscuits are pale golden and firm. Cool for 2 minutes and then lift the fingers off the baking tray with a palette knife on to a wire tray. Let them cool completely.

Blueberry cookies

Makes 12 cookies

79 calories per serving

Takes 15 minutes to prepare,
  15 minutes to cook

❄ (dough only)

75 g (2¾ oz) low fat spread

**5 tablespoons artificial
  sweetener**

1 egg, beaten

½ teaspoon vanilla extract

a pinch of salt

**175 g (6 oz) self raising flour,
  sifted**

grated zest of a lemon

**150 g (5½ oz) fresh
  blueberries**

*These gorgeous little cookies should be served in true
American style with a big glass of skimmed milk. The
uncooked cookie dough can be wrapped in cling film and
frozen for up to 3 months.*

1 Preheat the oven to Gas Mark 4/180°C/fan oven 160°C
and line two baking trays with non stick baking parchment.

2 Cream together the low fat spread and sweetener until light
and fluffy and then add the egg and vanilla extract and beat
again. Add the salt, flour and lemon zest and stir together until
you have a smooth dough.

3 Place tablespoons of the dough on to the baking trays,
spaced well apart, and shape each one into a round. Press
the blueberries into the top of the cookies and bake for
12–15 minutes, until golden. Cool on a wire rack.

Carrot cup cakes

Makes 9 cakes
128 calories per serving
Takes 12 minutes to prepare,
 17 minutes to cook

100 g (3½ oz) self raising flour
1 teaspoon baking powder
½ teaspoon ground cinnamon
50 g (1¾ oz) low fat spread
100 g (3½ oz) soft brown
 sugar
1 teaspoon vanilla extract
1 egg
2 tablespoons skimmed milk
1 small ripe banana, chopped
 roughly
1 carrot, peeled and grated
 coarsely
1 teaspoon icing sugar, for
 dusting

Carrot cake is one of the great tasting cake mixtures of all time. Grated carrot and ripe bananas add moistness, enabling you to have a healthier alternative without losing any of the flavour.

1 Preheat the oven to Gas Mark 5/190°C/fan oven 170°C. Line a bun tin with nine paper baking cases.

2 Put the flour, baking powder, cinnamon, low fat spread, sugar, vanilla extract, egg, milk and banana in a food processor and blend until smooth, scraping down the sides once or twice. If you don't have a food processor, mix well by hand in a large bowl.

3 Mix in the carrot, blending it in with short pulses of the food processor until just incorporated.

4 Spoon the mixture into the paper cases and bake for about 15–17 minutes until firm and springy on top.

5 Place the cakes on a wire rack and dust the tops with icing sugar.

Index